Teach Yourself VISUALLY™

OS X® Mavericks

Paul McFedries

Visual
A Wiley Brand

Teach Yourself Visually™ OS X® Mavericks

Published by
John Wiley & Sons, Inc.
10475 Crosspoint Boulevard
Indianapolis, IN 46256

www.wiley.com

Published simultaneously in Canada

Library of Congress Control Number: 2013939152

ISBN: 978-1-118-68323-1

Manufactured in the United States of America

10 9 8 7 6 5 4 3 2

Trademark Acknowledgments

Contact Us

For general information on our other products and services please contact our Customer Care Department within the U.S. at 877-762-2974, outside the U.S. at 317-572-3993 or fax 317-572-4002.

For technical support please visit www.wiley.com/techsupport.

Sales | Contact Wiley at (877) 762-2974 or fax (317) 572-4002.

Credits

Acquisitions Editor
Aaron Black

Project Editor
Jade L. Williams

Technical Editor
Dennis R. Cohen

Copy Editor
Kim Heusel

Editorial Director
Robyn Siesky

Business Manager
Amy Knies

Senior Marketing Manager
Sandy Smith

Vice President and Executive Group Publisher
Richard Swadley

Vice President and Executive Publisher
Barry Pruett

Project Coordinator
Sheree Montgomery

Graphics and Production Specialists
Andrea Hornberger
Jennifer Mayberry
Brent Savage

Quality Control Technician
Melissa Cossell

Proofreader
Linda Seifert

Indexer
Potomac Indexing, LLC

About the Author

Paul McFedries is a full-time technical writer. He has been authoring computer books since 1991 and has more than 85 books to his credit, including *Excel Data Analysis Visual Blueprint, Teach Yourself VISUALLY Excel 2013, Teach Yourself VISUALLY Windows 8, Windows 8 Visual Quick Tips, The Facebook Guide for People Over 50, iPhone 5 Portable Genius,* and *iPad 4th Generation and iPad mini Portable Genius,* all available from Wiley. Paul's books have sold more than 4 million copies worldwide. Paul is also the proprietor of Word Spy (`http://www.wordspy.com`), a website that tracks new words and phrases as they enter the English language. Paul invites you to drop by his personal website at `www.mcfedries.com`, or you can follow him on Twitter @paulmcf and @wordspy.

Author's Acknowledgments

It goes without saying that writers focus on text and I certainly enjoyed focusing on the text that you will read in this book. However, this book is more than just the usual collection of words and phrases designed to educate and stimulate the mind. A quick thumb through the pages will show you that this book is also chock full of treats for the eye, including copious screen shots, meticulous layouts, and sharp fonts. Those sure make for a beautiful book and that beauty comes from a lot of hard work by Wiley's immensely talented group of designers and layout artists.

They are all listed in the Credits section on the previous page, and I thank them for creating another gem. Of course, what you read in this book must also be accurate, logically presented, and free of errors. Ensuring all of this was an excellent group of editors that I got to work with directly, including project editor Jade Williams, copy editor Kim Heusel, and technical editor Dennis Cohen. Thanks to all of you for your exceptional competence and hard work. Thanks, as well, to Wiley Acquisitions Editor Aaron Black for asking me to write this book.

How to Use This Book

Who This Book Is For

This book is for the reader who has never used this particular technology or software application. It is also for readers who want to expand their knowledge.

The Conventions in This Book

1 Steps

This book uses a step-by-step format to guide you easily through each task. **Numbered steps** are actions you must do; **bulleted steps** clarify a point, step, or optional feature; and **indented steps** give you the result.

2 Notes

Notes give additional information — special conditions that may occur during an operation, a situation that you want to avoid, or a cross-reference to a related area of the book.

3 Icons and Buttons

Icons and buttons show you exactly what you need to click to perform a step.

4 Tips

Tips offer additional information, including warnings and shortcuts.

5 Bold

Bold type shows command names or options that you must click or text or numbers you must type.

6 Italics

Italic type introduces and defines a new term.

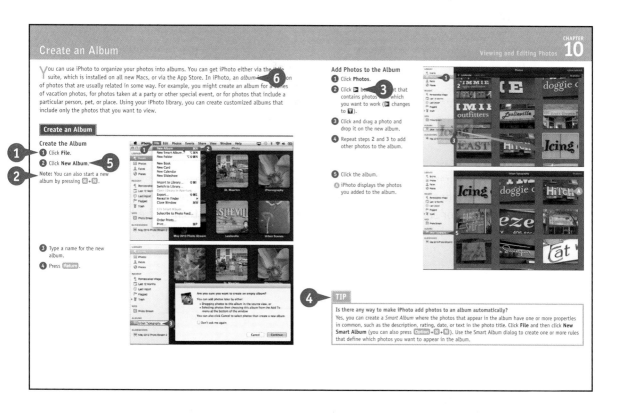

Table of Contents

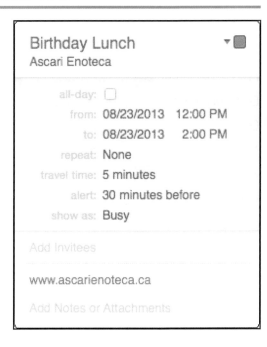

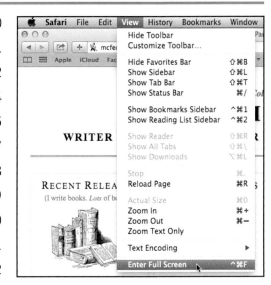

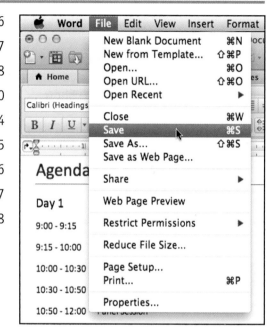

Table of Contents

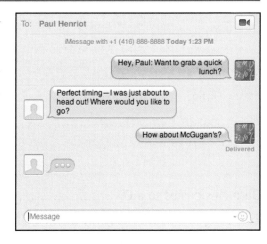

| Chapter 7 | Tracking Contacts and Events |

| Chapter 8 | Playing and Organizing Music |

Table of Contents

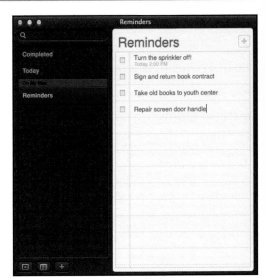

Table of Contents

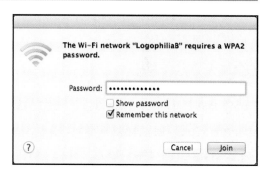

CHAPTER 1

Discovering What You Can Do with OS X

Are you ready to learn about what you can do with OS X? In this chapter, you find out about the wide variety of tasks you can perform with OS X, including creating documents; playing music; organizing photos, contacts, and appointments; and surfing the web.

Create Documents

Whether you use your Mac at home, at the office, or on the road, you can use OS X to create a wide variety of documents. In general, terms, a *document* is a file that contains information, which is usually text, but it may also consist of pictures, charts, lines, and other non-text items. With OS X, you can create documents such as lists, letters, memos, budgets, forecasts, presentations, and web pages.

Text Documents

You can use text-editing software on OS X to create simple documents such as lists, notes, instructions, and other items that do not require fonts, colors, or other types of formatting. With OS X, you can use the TextEdit application to create plain text documents, and the Notes application to create electronic notes.

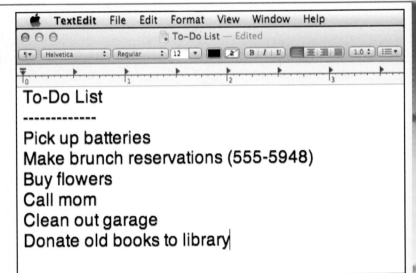

Word Processing Documents

You can use word processing software on OS X to create letters, resumes, memos, reports, newsletters, brochures, business cards, menus, flyers, invitations, and certificates. Anything that you use to communicate on paper, you can create using OS X. You can also use TextEdit to create formatted documents. Other examples include Microsoft Word for the Mac and Apple iWork Pages.

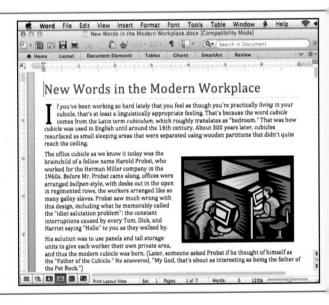

Spreadsheets

A spreadsheet application is a software program that enables you to manipulate numbers and formulas to quickly create powerful mathematical, financial, and statistical models. OS X comes with a test drive version of the Apple iWork Numbers application. Another example is Microsoft Excel for the Mac.

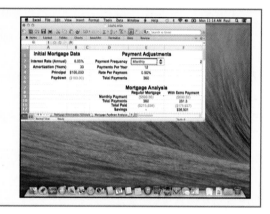

Presentations

A presentation program enables you to build professional-looking slides that you can use to convey your ideas to other people. OS X comes with a test drive version of the Apple iWork Keynote application. Another example is Microsoft PowerPoint for the Mac.

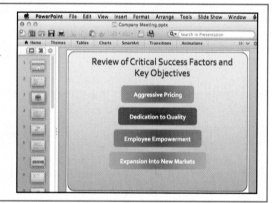

Web Pages

You can use web-page editing software on OS X to create your own pages to publish to the web. You can create a personal home page, a blog, or pages to support your business. OS X does not come with a program for creating web pages, but the App Store contains several excellent apps, including TextWrangler, BBEdit, and Web Form Builder Lite.

Play and Record Music

OS X is a veritable music machine that you can use to build, organize, play, and share your digital music collection. You can get music onto your Mac by copying it from audio CDs or by purchasing music online. If you are musically inclined, you can record or compose new tunes using an application called GarageBand (part of the Apple iLife suite). After you have a collection of music on your Mac, you can use OS X to create custom music CDs or copy some or all of the music to a device such as an iPod or iPad.

iTunes

OS X comes with the iTunes application, which stores your library of digital music files. With iTunes, you can play albums and songs, organize tunes into related playlists, download and edit track information, and organize your music to suit your style. You can also use iTunes to listen to Internet-based radio stations.

iTunes Store

You can use the iTunes application to connect directly to the online iTunes Store, where you can purchase individual songs, usually for 99 cents per song, or entire albums, usually for $9.99 per album. OS X downloads the purchased music to your iTunes library, and you can listen to the music on your Mac or add the music to your iPod, iPhone, or iPad.

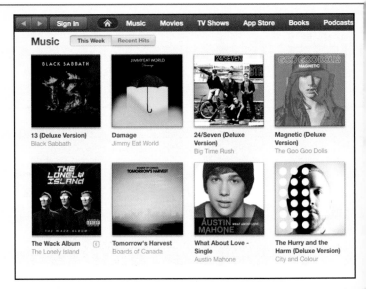

Import Music from a CD

If your Mac has a CD/DVD drive, you can add tracks from a music CD to the iTunes library. In iTunes, the process of copying tracks from a CD to your Mac is called *importing* or *ripping*. This enables you to listen to an album without inserting the CD into your drive each time.

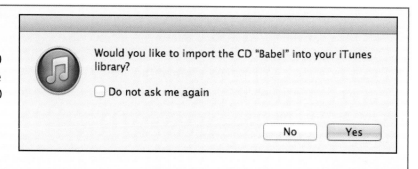

Record Music

If your Mac came with the iLife suite, then you can use the GarageBand program to record or compose your own tunes. You can attach an instrument such as a guitar or keyboard to your Mac and record your playing. You can also use GarageBand to add accompanying instruments such as drums, bass, piano, or another guitar.

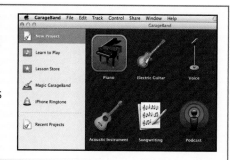

Burn Music to a CD

If your Mac has a CD/DVD burner, you can copy, or *burn*, music files from your Mac onto a CD. Burning CDs is a great way to create customized CDs that you can listen to on the computer or in a portable device. You can burn music files using the iTunes application.

Synchronize with an iPod, iPhone, or iPad

You can use the iTunes application to copy some or all of your music library to an iPod, iPhone, or iPad; this enables you to play your music wherever you are or on another audio device that connects to the device. When you attach the iPod, iPhone, or iPad to your Mac, iTunes automatically synchronizes the device according to the settings you specify.

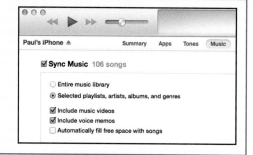

View and Organize Your Photos

Your Mac is perfect for showing your digital photos in their best light. OS X comes with tools that enable you to view individual photos and to run slide shows of multiple photos. OS X also enables you to organize your digital photos, import images from a digital camera or similar device (such as an iPhone or iPad), and edit your photos. Many Macs also come with a built-in camera that you can use to take simple snapshots.

View Photos

OS X gives you many ways to view your digital photos. You can view photos within Finder using the Cover Flow view, or by selecting the photos and pressing Spacebar. You can also double-click a photo file to open it using the Preview application, or you can open a file using the iPhoto application, if it is installed on your Mac. Also, both Preview and iPhoto enable you to run photo slide shows.

Organize Photos

If your Mac comes with iPhoto, part of the Apple iLife suite, you can use it to organize your collection of digital photos. For example, you can create albums of related photos, and you can create folders in which to store photos. You can also rename and rate photos, apply keywords to photos, flag important photos, and sort photos in various ways.

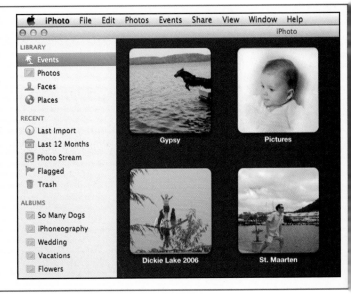

Import Photos to OS X

If you have a digital camera attached to your Mac, you can use either the Image Capture application or the iPhoto application, part of the Apple iLife suite, to import some or all of the camera's images to OS X.

Take Snapshots

If your Mac includes an iSight camera or has a digital video camera connected, you can use the Photo Booth application to take snapshots of whatever subject is currently displayed in the camera. You can also apply various effects to the photos.

Edit Photos

If your Mac comes with the iPhoto application, you can use it to edit your digital photos. You can rotate, crop, or straighten a photo; you can modify a photo's exposure, contrast, and sharpness; you can fix problems such as red eye and blemishes; and you can apply special effects to a photo.

Play and Make a Movie or Slide Show

Your Mac's solid graphical underpinnings mean that it is a great tool for video playback. For example, OS X comes with tools that enable you to watch movies on DVD. You can play digital video such as movies, TV shows, and podcast files that you download from the Internet, or digital video that you import from a camera. You can also use OS X to create your own digital movies and your own photo slide shows.

Play a DVD

If your Mac has a DVD drive, you can use the DVD Player application to play a DVD movie. You can either use full-screen mode to watch the movie using the entire screen, or watch the movie in a window while you work on other things. DVD Player has features that enable you to control the movie playback and volume.

Play a Video File

OS X comes with an application called QuickTime Player that enables you to open video files and control the playback and volume. QuickTime Player also includes many extra features, including the ability to record movies and audio, cut and paste scenes, and publish your videos on services such as YouTube and Facebook.

Play a Movie, TV Show, or Podcast

You most often use iTunes to play music, but you can also use it to play movies, video files stored on your Mac, and TV shows that you purchase from the iTunes Store, as well as podcasts that you download from the iTunes Store or subscribe to online.

Make a Movie

Most Macs come with an application called iMovie, part of the Apple iLife suite, which enables you to make your own digital movies. You can import clips from a video camera or video file, add clips to the movie, and rearrange and trim those clips as needed. You can also add transitions between scenes, music and sound effects, titles, and more.

Make a Slide Show

You can use OS X to create your own photo slide shows. Using the iPhoto application, part of the Apple iLife suite, you can create a slide show of your photos that includes animation effects, transition effects, and music. You can enhance the slide show with photo titles and sophisticated background and text themes.

Take Advantage of the Web

You can use OS X to connect to your Internet account. Once you establish the connection, you can use the built-in web browser to access almost any site that is available on the web. This means you can use your Mac to search for information, read the latest news, research and purchase goods and services, sell your own items, socialize with others, and more.

Surf the Web

OS X comes with a browser application called Safari that you use to surf the web. Safari offers several ways to load and navigate web pages. You can also use Safari to save your favorite web pages as bookmarks, view multiple pages in a single window using tabs, download files to your Mac, and much more.

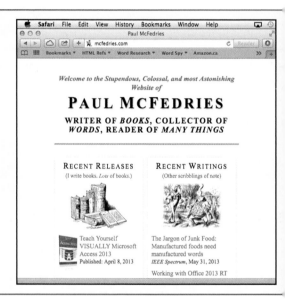

Search for Information

If you need information on a specific topic, free websites called *search engines* enable you to quickly search the web for pages that have the information you require. You can search the web either by going directly to a search engine site or by using the search feature built in to Safari.

Read News

The web is home to many sites that enable you to read the latest news. For example, many print sources have websites, some magazines exist only online, and there are more recent innovations such as blogs and RSS feeds. Some media sites require that you register to access the articles, but on most sites, the registration is free.

Buy and Sell

The online buying and selling of goods and services, or e-commerce, is a big part of the web. You can use web-based stores to purchase books, theater tickets, and even cars, which gives you the convenience of shopping at home, easily comparing prices and features, and having goods delivered to your door. Many sites also enable you to sell or auction your products or household items.

Socialize

The web offers many opportunities to socialize, whether you are looking for a friend or a date, or you just want some good conversation. However, it is a good idea to observe some common-sense precautions. For example, arrange to meet new friends in public places, supervise all online socializing done by children, and do not give out personal information to strangers.

Take Advantage of iCloud

You can use OS X to set up a free web-based iCloud account that enables you to perform many activities online, including exchanging e-mail, maintaining contacts, and tracking appointments. You can also use your iCloud account to synchronize data between your Mac and other Macs, Windows PCs, and devices such as iPod touches, iPhones, and iPads.

Communicate with Others

You can use OS X to communicate with other people using online and wireless technologies. For example, once you connect your Mac to the Internet, you can start sending and receiving e-mail, using either your Internet service provider (ISP) account or a web-based account. You can also use your Internet connection to exchange instant messages and perform audio and video chats. If you have a camera attached to your Mac, you can also place video calls to other people through your wired or wireless network.

Exchange E-mail

E-mail is the Internet system that enables you to electronically exchange messages with other Internet users anywhere in the world. To use e-mail, you must have an e-mail account, which is usually supplied by your ISP or e-mail service. The account gives you an e-mail address to which others can send messages. You then set up that account in the OS X Mail application.

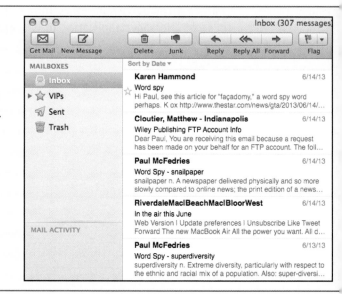

Exchange E-mail over the Web

You can also set up a web-based e-mail account. Although you can do this by using services such as Hotmail.com and Yahoo.com, many Mac users create iCloud accounts, which include web-based e-mail. A web-based account is convenient because it enables you to send and receive messages from any computer that has access to the Internet.

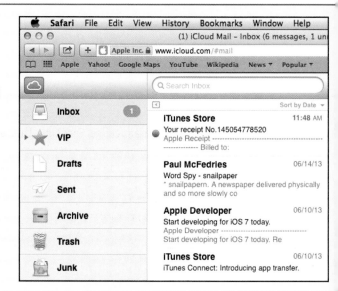

Exchange Instant Messages

Instant messaging allows you to contact other people who are online, thus enabling you to have a real-time exchange of messages. Communicating in real time means that if you send a message to another person who is online, that message appears on the person's computer right away. If that person sends you a response, it appears on your computer right away. In OS X Mavericks, you use the Messages application to exchange instant messages.

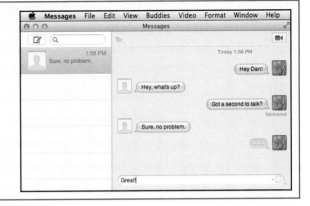

Share via Twitter

If you have an account on Twitter, you can configure OS X with your Twitter credentials. You can then share information with your Twitter followers by sending tweets from a number of OS X applications, including Safari and iPhoto. You can also use the Photo Booth application to take your picture, and then use that photo as your Twitter profile picture.

Place Video Calls

OS X Mavericks comes with a program called FaceTime that enables you to make video calls to other people. With a video call, your image is captured by a video camera — such as the iSight HD camera built in to many Macs — and a microphone captures your voice. Both the video and audio streams are sent to the other person, who could be using FaceTime on a Mac, an iPhone 4 or later, or an iPad 2 or later, or a 4th generation or newer iPod touch. The other person can also see and hear you.

Organize Your Contacts and Appointments

You can use OS X to help you organize various aspects of your life. For example, OS X comes with tools that enable you to enter, edit, organize, and work with your contacts, which means you can maintain a convenient digital version of your address book. Other OS X tools enable you to schedule events such as appointments, meetings, and trips. You can even configure OS X to synchronize your contacts and schedule among multiple devices.

Maintain Your Contact List

OS X comes with an application called Contacts that enables you to store information about your contacts. For each contact, you can store data such as the person's name, address, telephone number, e-mail address, and birthday.

Work with Contacts

You can use your Contacts list to perform many contact-related tasks. For example, you can use Mail to send a message either to individual contacts or to a contact group, which is a Contacts item that contains multiple contacts. Also, you can use Calendar to set up a meeting with one or more contacts.

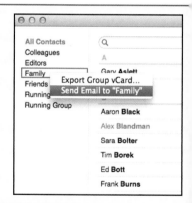

Schedule an Appointment

You can help organize your life by using OS X to record your appointments on the date and time they occur. You do this using the Calendar application, which uses an electronic calendar to store your appointments. You can even configure Calendar to display a reminder before an appointment occurs.

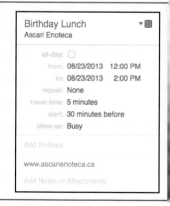

Schedule an All-Day Event

If an appointment has no set time — for example, a birthday, anniversary, or multiple-day event such as a sales meeting or vacation — you can use Calendar to set up the appointment as an all-day event.

Schedule a Repeating Appointment

If an appointment occurs regularly — for example, once a week or once every three months — you do not need to schedule every appointment manually. Instead, you can use Calendar to configure the activity as a repeating appointment, where you specify the repeat interval. Calendar then creates all the future appointments automatically.

Synchronize with iCloud

If you have an iCloud account, you can synchronize your OS X contacts and appointments so that they also appear in the iCloud Contacts and Calendar. If you have an iPod touch, iPhone, or iPad, you can use iCloud to sync those same contacts and appointments to your device. If you have a second Mac or a Windows PC, you can use iCloud to keep your contacts and appointments in sync on both computers.

CHAPTER 2

Learning Basic Program Tasks

One of the most crucial OS X concepts is the application (also sometimes called a program), because it is via applications that you perform all other OS X tasks. Therefore, it is important to have a basic understanding of how to start and manage applications in OS X.

Explore the OS X Screen

Before you can begin to understand how the OS X operating system works, you should become familiar with the basic screen elements. These elements include the OS X menu bar, the desktop, desktop icons, and the Dock. Understanding where these elements appear on the screen and what they are used for will help you work through the rest of the tasks in this book and will help you navigate OS X and its applications on your own.

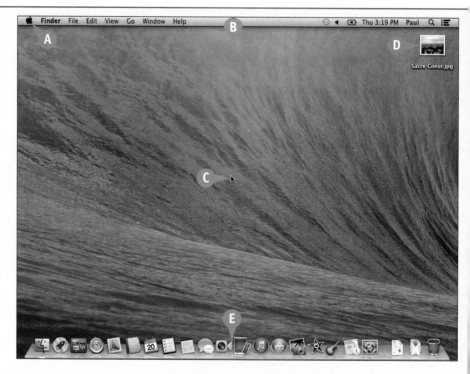

A Menu Bar

The menu bar contains the pull-down menus for OS X and most Mac software.

B Desktop

This is the OS X work area, where you work with your applications and documents.

C Mouse Pointer

When you move your mouse or move your finger on a trackpad, the pointer moves along with it.

D Desktop Icon

An icon on the desktop represents an application, a folder, a document, or a device attached to your Mac, such as a hard drive, a CD or DVD, or an iPod.

E Dock

The Dock contains several icons, each of which gives you quick access to a commonly used application.

Tour the Dock

The Dock is the strip that runs along the bottom of the Mac screen. The Dock is populated with several small images, which are called *icons*. Each icon represents a particular component of your Mac — an application, a folder, a document, and so on — and clicking the icon opens the component. This makes the Dock one of the most important and useful OS X features because it gives you one-click access to applications, folders, and documents. The icons shown here are typical, but your Mac may display a different arrangement.

A Finder

Work with the files on your computer.

B Launchpad

View, organize, and start your applications.

C Mission Control

Locate and navigate running applications.

D Safari

Browse the World Wide Web on the Internet.

E Mail

Send and receive e-mail messages.

F Contacts

Store and access people's names, addresses, and other contact information.

G Calendar

Record upcoming appointments, birthdays, meetings, and other events.

H Reminders

Set reminders for upcoming tasks.

I Notes

Record to-do lists and other short notes.

J Messages

Send instant messages to other people.

K FaceTime

Place video calls to other FaceTime users.

L Photo Booth

Take a picture using the camera on your Mac.

M iTunes

Play music and other media and add media to your iPod, iPhone, or iPad.

N App Store

Install new applications and upgrade existing ones.

O iPhoto

Import and edit digital photos and other images.

P iMovie

Import video footage and edit your own digital movies.

Q GarageBand

Create songs, podcasts, and other audio files.

R Maps

Find and get directions to locations.

S System Preferences

Customize and configure your Mac.

T Documents

Display the contents of your Documents folder.

U Downloads

Display the contents of your Downloads folder.

V Trash

Delete files, folders, and applications.

Start an Application

To perform tasks of any kind in OS X, you use one of the applications installed on your Mac. The application you use depends on the task you want to perform. For example, if you want to surf the World Wide Web, you use a web browser application, such as the Safari program that comes with OS X. Before you can use an application, however, you must first tell OS X which application you want to run. OS X launches the application and displays it on the desktop. You can then use the application's tools to perform your tasks.

Start an Application

1 Click the **Finder** icon ( ).

Note: If the application that you want to start has an icon in the Dock, you can click the icon to start the application and skip the steps in this section.

The Finder window appears.

2 Click **Applications**.

Note: You can also navigate to Applications in any Finder window by pressing **Shift**+**⌘**+**A** or by choosing **Go** and then clicking **Applications**.

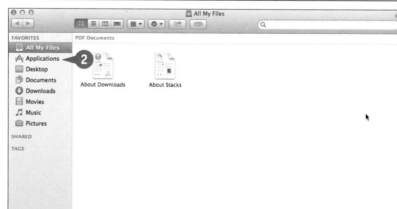

The Applications window appears.

③ Double-click the icon of the application that you want to start.

Note: If you see a folder icon (📁), it means that the application resides in its own folder, which is a storage area on the computer. Double-click 📁 to open the folder and then double-click the application icon.

Ⓐ The application appears on the desktop.

Ⓑ OS X adds a button for the application to the Dock.

Ⓒ The menu bar displays the menus associated with the application.

Note: Another common way to launch an application is to use Finder to locate a document with which you want to work, and then double-click that document.

TIPS

How do I add an icon to the Dock for an application I use frequently?

To add an icon to the desktop, repeat steps **1** to **3** in this task. Right-click the application's Dock icon, click **Options**, and then click **Keep in Dock**.

How do I shut down a running application?

To shut down a running application, right-click the application's Dock icon and then click **Quit**. Alternatively, you can switch to the application and press ⌘+Q.

Start an Application Using Launchpad

You can start an application using the Launchpad feature. This is often faster than using the Applications folder, particularly for applications that do not have a Dock icon.

Launchpad is designed to mimic the Home screens of the iPhone, iPad, and iPod touch. So if you own one or more of these devices, then you are already familiar with how Launchpad works.

Start an Application Using Launchpad

1 Click the **Launchpad** icon ( ).

The Launchpad screen appears.

2 If the application you want to start resides in a different Launchpad screen, click the dot that corresponds to the screen.

Launchpad switches to the
screen and displays the
applications.

 If the application you want
to start resides within a
folder, click the folder.

Launchpad opens the folder.

4 Click the icon of the
application you want
to start.

OS X starts the application.

Is there an easier way to navigate the Launchpad screens?
Yes. OS X has designed Launchpad to work like the iPhone, iPad, and iPod touch, which you navigate by
using a finger to swipe the screen right or left. With your Mac, you can also navigate the Launchpad screens
by swiping. In this case, however, you must use two fingers, and you swipe right or left on either the
trackpad or the surface of a Magic Mouse. You can also use a trackpad gesture to open Launchpad: Place
four fingers lightly on the trackpad and pinch them together.

Switch Between Applications

If you plan on running multiple applications at the same time, you need to know how to easily switch from one application to another. In OS X, after you start one application, you do not need to close that application before you open another one. OS X supports a feature called *multitasking*, which means running two or more applications at once. This is handy if you need to use several applications throughout the day.

Switch Between Applications

1 Click the Dock icon of the application to which you want to switch.

Ⓐ OS X brings the application window(s) to the foreground.

Ⓑ The menu bar displays the menus associated with the application.

Note: To switch between applications from the keyboard, press and hold ⌘ and repeatedly press Tab until the application that you want is highlighted in the list of running applications. Release ⌘ to switch to the application.

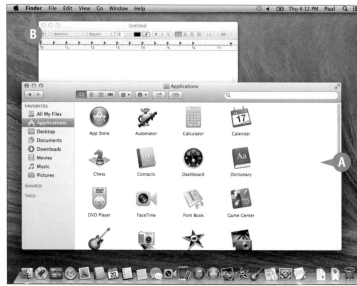

View Running Applications with Mission Control

The Mission Control feature makes it easier for you to navigate and locate your running applications. OS X allows you to open multiple applications at once, and the only real limit to the number of open applications you can have is the amount of memory contained in your Mac. In practical terms, this means you can easily open several applications, some of which may have multiple open windows. To help locate and navigate to the window you need, use the Mission Control feature.

View Running Applications with Mission Control

1 Click **Mission Control** (⊞).

Note: You can also invoke Mission Control by pressing F3 or by placing three fingers on the trackpad of your Mac and then swiping up.

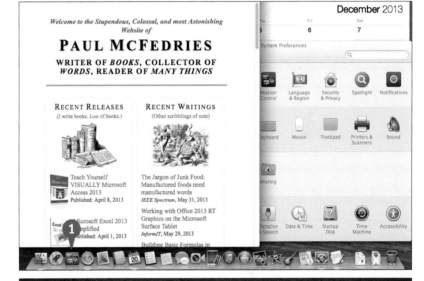

A Mission Control displays each open window.

B Mission Control groups windows from the same application.

To switch to a particular window, click it.

C To close Mission Control without selecting a window, click **Desktop** or press Esc.

Tour an Application Window

When you start an application, it appears on the OS X desktop in its own window. Each application has a unique window layout, but almost all application windows have a few features in common. To get the most out of your applications and to start working quickly and efficiently in an application, you need to know what these common features are and where to find them within the application window.

Ⓐ Close Button

Click the **Close** button (Ⓞ) to remove the application window from the desktop, usually without exiting the application.

Ⓑ Minimize Button

Click the **Minimize** button (Ⓞ) to remove the window from the desktop and display an icon for the currently open document in the right side of the Dock. The window is still open, but not active.

Ⓒ Zoom Button

Click the **Zoom** button (Ⓞ) to enlarge the window so that it can display all of its content, or as much of its content as can fit the screen.

Ⓓ Toolbar

The toolbar contains buttons that offer easy access to common application commands and features, although not all applications have toolbars. To move the window, click and drag the toolbar.

Ⓔ Status Bar

The status bar displays information about the current state of the application or document.

Ⓕ Vertical Scroll Bar

Click and drag the vertical scroll bar to navigate up and down in a document. In some cases, you can also click and drag the horizontal scroll bar to navigate left and right in a document.

Ⓖ Resize Control

Click and drag any edge or corner of the window to make the window larger or smaller.

Run an Application Full Screen

You can maximize the viewing and working areas of an application by running that application in full-screen mode. When you switch to full-screen mode, OS X hides the menu bar, the application's status bar, the Dock, and the top section of the application window (the section that includes the Close, Minimize, and Zoom buttons). OS X then expands the rest of the application window so that it takes up the entire screen. You must be running OS X Lion or later to use full-screen mode. Note, too, that not all programs are capable of switching to full-screen mode.

Run an Application Full Screen

1 Click **View**.

2 Click **Enter Full Screen**.

You can also press
`Control` + `⌘` + `F`.

A You can also click **Full Screen** (⬈).

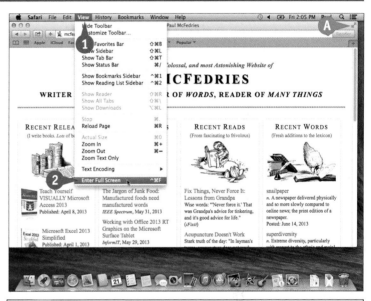

OS X expands the application window to take up the entire screen.

Note: To exit full-screen mode, move the mouse ▶ up to the top of the screen to reveal the menu bar, click **View**, and then click **Exit Full Screen**. You can also press `Control` + `⌘` + `F`.

Select a Command from a Pull-Down Menu

When you are working in an application, you can use the menu bar to access the application's commands and features. Each item in the menu bar represents a *pull-down menu*, a collection of commands usually related to each other in some way. For example, the File menu commands usually deal with file-related tasks such as opening and closing documents. The items in a menu are either commands that execute an action in the application, or features that you can turn on and off.

Select a Command from a Pull-Down Menu

Execute Commands

1 Click the name of the menu that you want to display.

A The application displays the menu.

2 Click the command that you want to execute.

The application executes the command.

B If a command is followed by an ellipsis (...), it means the command displays a dialog.

C If a command is followed by an arrow (▶), it means the command displays a submenu. Click the command to open the submenu and then click the command that you want to run.

Turn Features On and Off

1 Click the name of the menu that you want to display.

D The application displays the menu.

2 Click the menu item.

The application turns the feature either on or off.

Select a Command Using a Toolbar

Y ou can access many application commands faster by using the toolbar. Many applications come with a toolbar, which is a collection of buttons, lists, and other controls displayed in a strip, usually across the top of the application window. Because the toolbar is always visible, you can always use it to select commands, which means that the toolbar often gives you one-click access to the application's most common features. This is faster than using the menu bar method, which often takes several clicks, depending on the command.

Select a Command Using a Toolbar

Turn Features On and Off

1 Click the toolbar button that represents the feature you want to turn on.

A The application turns the feature on and indicates this state by highlighting the toolbar button.

B When a feature is turned off, the application does not highlight the button.

Execute Commands

1 Click the toolbar button that represents the command that you want.

2 If the button displays a menu, click the command on the menu.

C The application executes the command.

Select Options with Dialog Controls

You often interact with an application by selecting options or typing text using a dialog. A *dialog* is a small window that appears when an application has information for you, or needs you to provide information. For example, when you select the File menu's Print command to print a document, you use the Print dialog to specify the number of copies that you want to print.

You provide that and other information by accessing various types of dialog controls. To provide information to an application quickly and accurately, you need to know what these dialog controls look like and how they work.

ⓐ Command Button

Clicking a command button executes the command printed on the button face. For example, you can click **OK** to apply settings that you have chosen in a dialog, or you can click **Cancel** to close the dialog without changing the settings.

ⓑ Text Box

A text box enables you to enter typed text. Press Delete to delete any existing characters, and then type your text.

ⓒ List Box

A list box displays a list of choices from which you select the item you want. Use the vertical scroll bar to bring the item you want into view, and then click the item to select it.

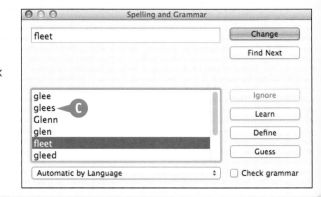

ⓓ Tabs

Many dialogs offer a large number of controls, so related controls appear on different tabs, and the tab names and icons appear across the top of the dialog. Click a tab to see its controls.

ⓔ Pop-Up Menu

A pop-up menu displays a list of choices from which you select the item you want. Click the up-down arrows (⌄) to display the menu, and then click the item that you want to select.

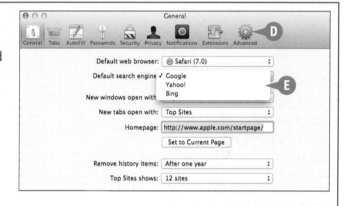

ⓕ Check Box

Clicking a check box toggles an application feature on and off. If you are turning on a feature, the check box changes from ☐ to ☑; if you are turning off the feature, the check box changes from ☑ to ☐.

ⓖ Radio Button

Clicking a radio button turns on an application feature. Only one radio button in a group can be turned on at a time. When you click a radio button that is currently off, it changes from ◯ to ◉; a radio button that is on changes from ◉ to ◯.

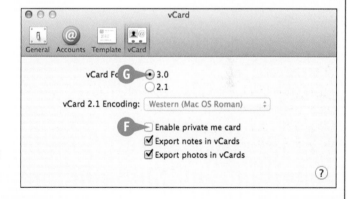

CHAPTER 3

Learning Basic Document Tasks

Much of the work you do in OS X involves documents, which are files that contain text, images, and other data. These tasks include saving, opening, printing, and editing documents, as well as copying and renaming files.

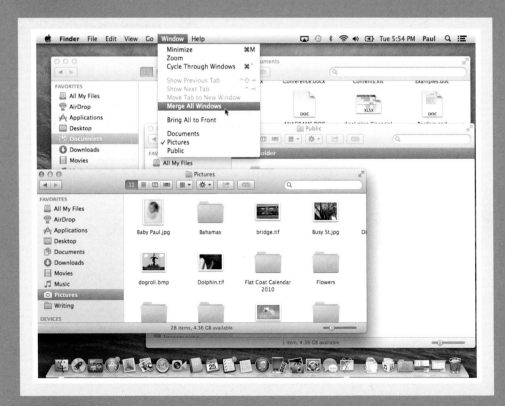

Save a Document

After you create a document and make changes to it, you can save the document to preserve your work. When you work on a document, OS X stores the changes in your computer's memory. However, OS X erases the contents of the Mac's memory each time you shut down or restart the computer. This means that the changes you make to your document are lost when you turn off or restart your Mac. However, saving the document preserves your changes on your Mac's hard drive.

Save a Document

1 Click **File**.

2 Click **Save**.

In most applications, you can also press ⌘+S.

If you have saved the document previously, your changes are now preserved, and you do not need to follow the rest of the steps in this section.

If this is a new document that you have never saved before, the Save As dialog appears.

3 Type the filename you want to use in the Save As text box.

Ⓐ To store the file in a different folder, you can click the **Where** ⁝ and then select the location that you prefer from the pop-up menu.

4 Click **Save**.

The application saves the file.

Open a Document

To work with a document that you have saved in the past, you can open it in the application that you used to create it. When you save a document, you save its contents to your Mac's hard drive, and those contents are stored in a separate file. When you open the document using the same application that you used to save it, OS X loads the file's contents into memory and displays the document in the application. You can then view or edit the document as needed.

Open a Document

1 Start the application with which you want to work.

2 Click **File**.

3 Click **Open**.

In most applications, you can also press ⌘+O.

The Open dialog appears.

A To select a different folder from which to open a file, you can click ⁝ and then click the location that you prefer.

4 Click the document.

5 Click **Open**.

The document appears in a window on the desktop.

Print a Document

When you need a hard copy of your document, either for your files or to distribute to someone else, you can send the document to your printer. Most applications that deal with documents also come with a Print command. When you run this command, the Print dialog appears. You use the Print dialog to choose the printer you want to use, as well as to specify how many copies you want to print. Many Print dialogs also enable you to see a preview of your document before printing it.

Print a Document

1. Turn on your printer.

2. Open the document that you want to print.

3. Click **File**.

4. Click **Print**.

In many applications, you can select the Print command by pressing ⌘+P.

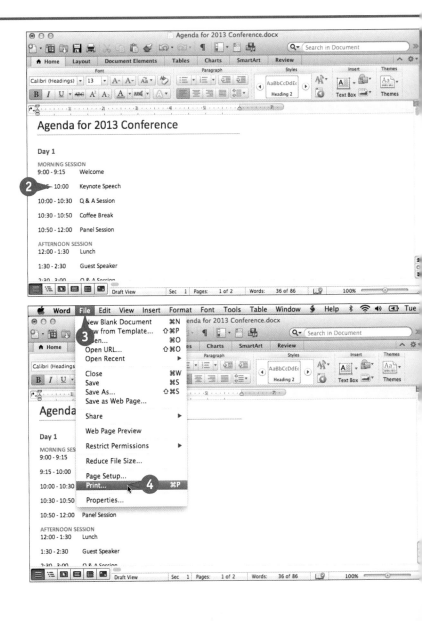

The Print dialog appears.

The layout of the Print dialog varies from application to application. The version shown here is a typical example.

5 If you have more than one printer, click ✦ in the Printer list to select the printer that you want to use.

6 To print more than one copy, type the number of copies to print in the Copies text box to.

7 Click **Print**.

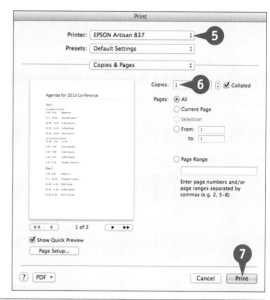

A OS X prints the document. The printer's icon appears in the Dock while the document prints.

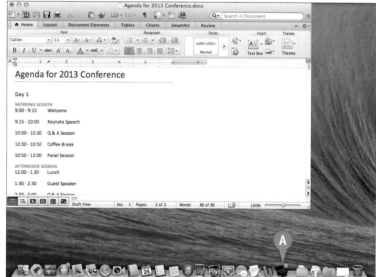

TIP

Can I print only part of my document?

Yes, you can print a range of pages by selecting the **From** option (◯ changes to ◉) and then using the two text boxes to type the numbers of the first and last pages you want to print.

If you just want to print one page, click anywhere within the page before running the Print command; then select the **Current Page** option (◯ changes to ◉) or click **From** (◯ changes to ◉) and type the page number in both text boxes.

If you just want to print a section of the document, select the text before running the Print command, and then select the **Selection** option (◯ changes to ◉).

Edit Document Text

When you work with a character-based file, such as a text or word processing document or an e-mail message, you need to know the basic techniques for editing text. It is rare that any text you type in a document is perfect the first time through. It is more likely that the text contains errors that require correcting, or words, sentences, or paragraphs that appear in the wrong place. To get your document text the way you want it, you need to know how to edit text, including deleting characters, selecting the text with which you want to work, and copying and moving text.

Edit Document Text

Delete Characters

1 In a text document, click immediately to the right of the last character that you want to delete.

A The cursor appears after the character.

Agenda for 2013 Conference

Day 1

MORNING SESSION
9:00 - 9:15	Welcome
9:15 - 10:00	Keynote Speech
10:00 - 10:30	Q & A Session
10:30 - 10:50	Coffee Break
10:50 - 12:00	Panel Session
12:00 - 1:30	Lunch

AFTERNOON SESSION
1:30 - 2:30	Guest Speaker
2:30 - 3:00	Q & A Session
3:00 - 3:20	Coffeee Break
3:20 - 4:00	A Look at the Future
4:00 - 5:00	Breakout Sessions

1

A

2 Press **Delete** until you have deleted all the characters you want.

If you make a mistake, immediately click **Edit**, and then click **Undo**. You can also press ⌘+Z.

Agenda for 2013 Conference

Day 1

MORNING SESSION
9:00 - 9:15	Welcome
9:15 - 10:00	Keynote Speech
10:00 - 10:30	Q & A Session
10:30 - 10:50	Coffee Break
10:50 - 12:00	Panel Session
12:00 - 1:30	Lunch

AFTERNOON SESSION
1:30 - 2:30	Guest Speaker
2:30 - 3:00	Q & A Session
3:00 - 3:20	Coffeee Break
3:20 - 4:00	A Look at the Future
4:00 - 5:00	Breakout Sessions

2

Select Text for Editing

1 Click and drag across the text that you want to select.

2 Release the mouse button.

B The application highlights the selected text.

Agenda for 2013 Conference

Day 1

MORNING SESSION ◀ **1**

9:00 - 9:15	Welcome
9:15 - 10:00	Keynote Speech
10:00 - 10:30	Q & A Session
10:30 - 10:50	Coffee Break
10:50 - 12:00	Panel Session
12:00 - 1:30	Lunch

AFTERNOON SESSION

Word File Edit View Insert Format Font Tools Table Window Help

Agenda for 2013 Conference.docx

150% ▾ Q▾ Search in Doc

Home | Layout | Document Elements | Tables | Charts | SmartArt | Review

Agenda for 2013 Conference

2 **Day 1**

MORNING SESSION ◀ **B**

9:00 - 9:15	Welcome
9:15 - 10:00	Keynote Speech
10:00 - 10:30	Q & A Session
10:30 - 10:50	Coffee Break
10:50 - 12:00	Panel Session
12:00 - 1:30	Lunch

TIP

Are there any shortcut methods for selecting text?

Yes, most OS X applications have shortcuts you can use. Here are the most useful ones:

Double-click a word to select it.

- Press and hold **Shift** and press ➡ or ⬅ to select entire words.
- Press and hold **Shift** and ⌘ and press ➡ to select to the end of the line, or ⬅ to select to the beginning of the line.

Triple-click inside a paragraph to select it.

Click **Edit** and then click **Select All**, or press ⌘+**A** to select the entire document.

continued ▶ **41**

Edit Document Text (continued)

Once you select text, you can then copy or move the text to another location in your document. Copying text is often a useful way to save work. For example, if you want to use the same passage of text elsewhere in the document, you can copy it instead of typing it from scratch. If you need a similar passage in another part of the document, copy the original and then edit the copy as needed. If you type a passage of text in the wrong position within the document, you can fix that by moving the text to the correct location.

Edit Document Text (continued)

Copy Text

1. Select the text that you want to copy.

2. Click **Edit**.

3. Click **Copy**.

   In most applications, you can also press ⌘+C.

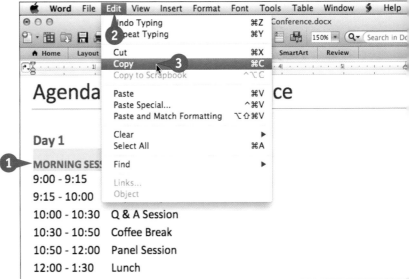

4. Click inside the document where you want the copied text to appear.

   The cursor appears in the position where you clicked.

5. Click **Edit**.

6. Click **Paste**.

   In most applications, you can also press ⌘+V.

Ⓐ The application inserts a copy of the selected text at the cursor position.

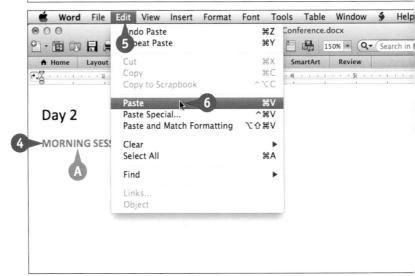

42

Move Text

① Select the text that you want to move.

② Click **Edit**.

③ Click **Cut**.

In most applications, you can also press ⌘+X.

The application removes the text from the document.

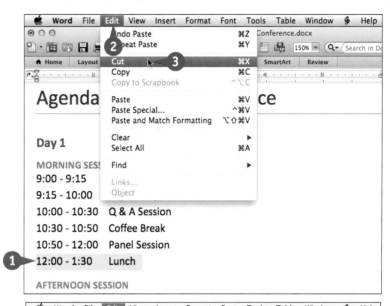

④ Click inside the document where you want to move the text.

The cursor appears at the position where you clicked.

⑤ Click **Edit**.

⑥ Click **Paste**.

In most applications, you can also press ⌘+V.

Ⓑ The application inserts the text at the cursor position.

TIP

How do I move and copy text with my mouse?

To move and copy text with your mouse, select the text that you want to move or copy. To move the selected text, position the mouse pointer over the selection and then click and drag the text to the new position within the document.

To copy the selected text, position the mouse pointer over the selection, press and hold the Option key, and then click and drag the text (the mouse ➤ changes to ➤) to the new position within the document.

Copy a File

You can use OS X to make an exact copy of a file. This is useful when you want to make an extra copy of an important file to use as a backup. Similarly, you might require a copy of a file if you want to send the copy on a disk to another person. Finally, copying a file is also a real timesaver if you need a new file very similar to an existing file: You copy the original file and then make the required changes to the copy. You can copy either a single file or multiple files. You can also use this technique to copy a folder.

Copy a File

1 Locate the file that you want to copy.

2 Open the folder to which you want to copy the file.

To open a second folder window, click **File** and then click **New Finder Window**, or press ⌘+N.

3 Press and hold the Option key, and then click and drag the file and drop it inside the destination folder.

A The original file remains in its folder.

B A copy of the original file appears in the destination folder.

You can also make a copy of a file in the same folder, which is useful if you want to make major changes to the file and you would like to preserve a copy of the original. Click the file, click **File**, and then click **Duplicate**, or press ⌘+D. OS X creates a copy with the word "copy" added to the filename.

44

Move a File

When you need to store a file in a new location, the easiest way is to move the file from its current folder to another folder on your Mac. When you save a file for the first time, you specify a folder on your Mac's hard drive. This original location is not permanent, however. Using the technique in this section, you can move the file to another location on your Mac's hard drive. You can use this technique to move a single file, multiple files, and even a folder.

Move a File

1 Locate the file that you want to move.

2 Open the folder to which you want to move the file.

To create a new destination folder in the current folder, click **File** and then click **New Folder**, or press **Shift**+**⌘**+**N**.

3 Click and drag the file and drop it inside the destination folder.

Note: If you are moving the file to another drive, you must hold down ⌘ while you click and drag the file.

Ⓐ The file disappears from its original folder.

Ⓑ The file moves to the destination folder.

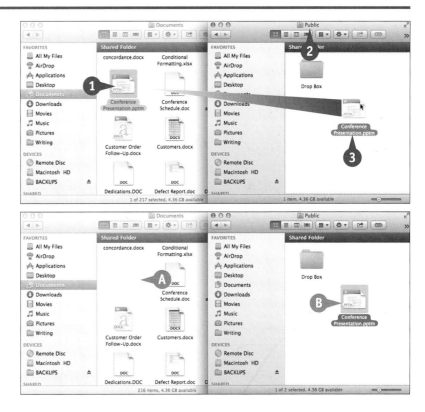

Rename a File

You can change the name of a file, which is useful if the current filename does not accurately describe the contents of the file. Giving your document a descriptive name makes it easier to find the file later. You should rename only those documents that you have created or that have been given to you by someone else. Do not try to rename any of the OS X system files or any files associated with your applications, or your computer may behave erratically or even crash.

Rename a File

1 Open the folder containing the file that you want to rename.

2 Click the file.

3 Press **Return**.

A A text box appears around the filename.

You can also rename any folders that you have created.

4 Edit the existing name or type a new name that you want to use for the file.

If you decide that you do not want to rename the file after all, you can press **Esc** to cancel the operation.

5 Press **Return** or click an empty section of the folder.

B The new name appears under the file icon.

Delete a File

When you no longer need a file, you can delete it. This helps to prevent your hard drive from becoming cluttered with unnecessary files. You should ensure that you delete only those documents that you have created or that have been given to you by someone else. Do not delete any of the OS X system files or any files associated with your applications, or your computer may behave erratically or even crash.

Delete a File

1 Locate the file that you want to delete.

2 Click and drag the file and drop it on the Trash icon in the Dock.

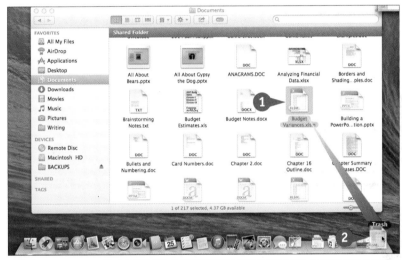

A The file disappears from the folder.

You can also delete a file by clicking it and then pressing ⌘ + Delete.

If you delete a file accidentally, you can restore it. In the dock, click the **Trash** icon to open the Trash window. Right-click the file and then click **Put Back**.

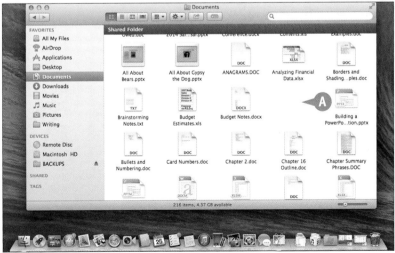

Open a Folder in a Tab

You can make it easier to work with multiple folders simultaneously by opening each folder in its own tab within a single Finder window. As you work with your documents, you may come upon one or more folders that you want to keep available while you work with other folders. Instead of cluttering the desktop with multiple Finder windows, OS X enables you to use a single Finder window that displays each open folder in a special section of the window called a *tab*. To view the contents of any open folder, you need only click its tab.

Open a Folder in a Tab

Open a Folder in a New Tab

1. Right-click the folder you want to open.

2. Click **Open in New Tab**.

A. A new tab appears for the folder.

B. The folder's contents appear here.

C. Click any tab to display its contents in the Finder window.

D. To close a tab, move the mouse ▸ over the tab and then click **Close Tab** (⊠).

Create a New Tab

① Click **File**.

② Click **New Tab**.

Ⓔ If you already have two or more tabs open, you can also click the **Create a new tab** icon (✚).

Finder creates a new tab.

Merge Open Folder Windows into Tabs

① Click **Window**.

② Click **Merge All Windows**.

Finder moves all the open folder windows into tabs in a single Finder window.

Note: To copy or move a file to a folder open in another tab, click and drag the file from its current folder and drop it on the other folder's tab.

TIP

Are there any shortcuts I can use to work with folders in tabs?

Yes, here are a few useful keyboard techniques you can use:

- In a folder, press and hold ⌘ and double-click a subfolder to open it in a tab. Press and hold ⌘+Shift instead to open the subfolder in a tab without switching to the tab.
- In the sidebar, press and hold ⌘ (or ⌘+Shift) and click a folder to open it in a tab.
- Press Shift+⌘+] or Shift+⌘+[to cycle through the tabs.
- Press ⌘+W to close the current tab.
- Press Option and click ⊠ to close every tab but the one you clicked.

CHAPTER 4

Browsing the Web

If your Mac is connected to the Internet, you can use the Safari browser to navigate, or *surf*, websites. Safari offers features that make it easier to browse the web. For example, you can open multiple pages in a single Safari window and you can save your favorite sites for easier access.

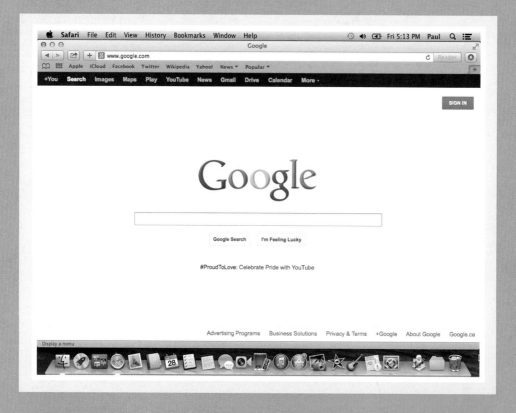

Select a Link

Almost all web pages include links to other pages that contain related information. When you select a link, your web browser loads the other page. Web page links come in two forms: text and images. Text links consist of a word or phrase that usually appears underlined and in a different color from the rest of the page text. However, web page designers can control the look of their links, so text links may not always stand out in this way. Therefore, knowing which words, phrases, or images are links is not always obvious. The only way to tell for sure is to position the mouse over the text or image; if the mouse changes to a pointing finger, you know the item is a link.

Select a Link

1 In the Dock, click the **Safari** icon (⬤).

2 Position the mouse ➤ over the link (➤ changes to 👆).

3 Click the text or image.

Ⓐ The status bar shows the address of the linked page.

Note: The address shown in the status bar when you point at a link may be different from the one shown when the page is downloading. This occurs when the website *redirects* the link.

Note: If you do not see the status bar, click **View** and then click **Show Status Bar**.

The linked web page appears.

Ⓑ The web page title and address change after the linked page is loaded.

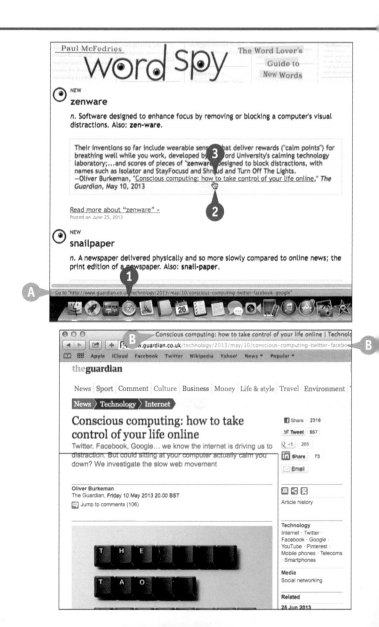

Enter a Web Page Address

Every web page is uniquely identified by an address called the Uniform Resource Locator, or URL. You can type the address into the web browser to display the page.

The URL is composed of four parts: the *transfer method* (usually HTTP, which stands for Hypertext Transfer Protocol), the *domain name*, the *directory* where the web page is located on the server, and the *filename*. The domain name suffix most often used is .com (commercial), but other common suffixes include .gov (government), .org (nonprofit organization), .edu (education), and country domains such as .ca (Canada).

Enter a Web Page Address

1 Click inside the address bar.

2 Press **Delete** to delete the existing address.

3 Type the address of the web page you want to visit.

4 Press **Return**.

A You can also click the site if it appears in the list of suggested sites.

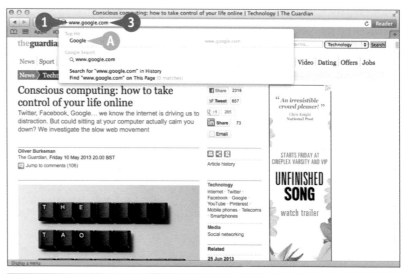

The web page appears.

B The web page title changes after the page is loaded.

Open a Web Page in a Tab

You can make it easier to work with multiple web pages and sites simultaneously by opening each page in its own tab. As you surf the web, you may come upon a page that you want to keep available while you visit other sites. Instead of leaving the page and trying to find it again when you need it, Safari lets you leave the page open in a special section of the browser window called a *tab*. You can then use a second tab to visit your other sites, and to resume viewing the first site, you need only click its tab.

Open a Web Page in a Tab

Open a Link in a New Tab

① Right-click the link you want to open.

② Click **Open Link in New Tab**.

Ⓐ A new tab appears with the page title.

③ Click the tab to display the page.

Create a New Tab

1 Click **File**.

2 Click **New Tab**.

B If you already have two or more tabs open, you can also click the **Create a new tab** icon ( ).

C Safari creates a new tab and displays the Top Sites page.

After you have used Safari for a while, the Top Sites page lists the websites that you have visited most often.

3 Type the address of the page you want to load into the new tab.

4 Press **Return**.

D Safari displays the page in the tab.

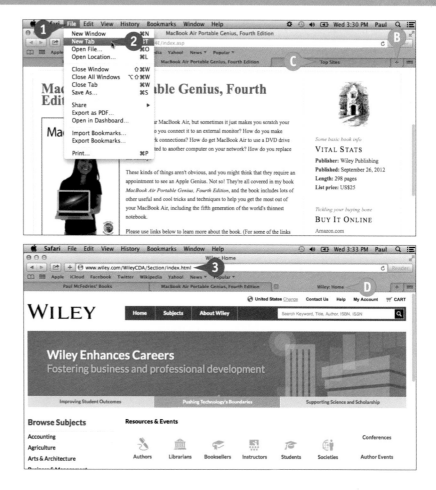

TIP

Are there any shortcuts I can use to open web pages in tabs?

Yes, here are a few useful keyboard techniques you can use:

- Press and hold ⌘ and click a link to open the page in a tab.
- Type an address and then press ⌘+**Return** to open the page in a new tab.
- Press **Shift**+⌘+**]** or **Shift**+⌘+**[** to cycle through the tabs.
- Press ⌘+**W** to close the current tab.

Navigate Web Pages

After you have visited several pages, you can return to a page you visited earlier. Instead of retyping the address or looking for the link, Safari gives you some easier methods. When you navigate from page to page, you create a kind of path through the web. Safari keeps track of this path by maintaining a list of the pages you visit. You can use that list to go back to a page you have visited. After you go back to a page you have visited, you can use the same list to go forward through the pages again.

Navigate Web Pages

Go Back One Page

1 Click the **Previous Page** icon (◀).

The previous page you visited appears.

Go Back Several Pages

1 Click and hold down the mouse ▶ on ◀.

Note: The list of visited pages is different for each tab that you have open. If you do not see the page you want, you may need to click a different tab.

A list of the pages you have visited appears.

2 Click the page you want to revisit.

The page appears.

Go Forward One Page

1 Click the **Next Page** icon (▶).

The next page appears.

Note: If you are at the last page viewed up to that point, ▶ is not active.

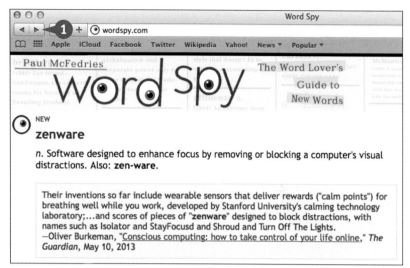

Go Forward Several Pages

1 Click and hold down ▶ on ▶ .

A list of the pages you have visited appears.

Note: The list of visited pages is different for each tab that you have open. If you do not see the page you want, you may need to click a different tab.

2 Click the page you want to revisit.

The page appears.

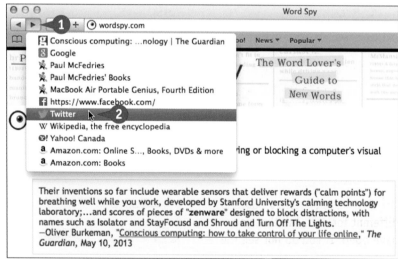

Are there any shortcuts I can use to navigate web pages?
Yes, a few useful keyboard shortcuts you can use are

- Press ⌘+[to go back one page.
- Press ⌘+] to go forward one page.
- Press Shift+⌘+H to return to the Safari home page (the first page you see when you open Safari).

Navigate with the History List

The Previous Page and Next Page buttons (◄ and ►) enable you to navigate pages in the current browser session. To redisplay sites that you have visited in the past few days or weeks, you need to use the History list, which is a collection of the websites and pages you have visited over the past month.

If you visit sensitive places such as an Internet banking site or your corporate site, you can increase security by clearing the history list so that other people cannot see where you have been.

Navigate with the History List

Load a Page from the History List

1 Click **History**.

2 Click the date when you visited the page.

A submenu of pages that you visited during that day appears.

3 Click the page you want to revisit.

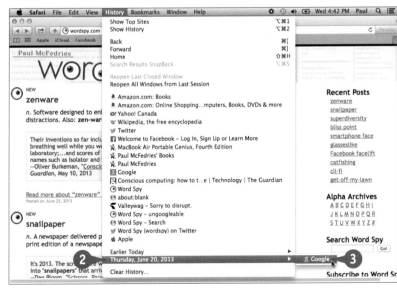

Ⓐ The page appears.

Clear the History List

1 Click **History**.

2 Click **Clear History**.

Safari deletes all the pages from the history list.

How can I control the length of time that Safari keeps track of the pages I visit?

1 In the menu bar, click **Safari**.

2 Click **Preferences**.

3 Click **General**.

4 Click the **Remove history items** pop-up menu (‡) and then select the amount of time you want Safari to track your history.

5 Click ⊙.

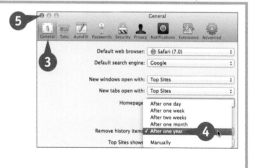

Change Your Home Page

Your home page is the web page that appears when you first start Safari. The default home page is usually the Apple.com Start page, but you can change that to any other page you want, or even to an empty page. This is useful if you do not use the Apple.com Start page, or if there is another page that you always visit at the start of your browsing session. For example, if you have your own website, it might make sense to always begin there. Safari also comes with a command that enables you to view the home page at any time during your browsing session.

Change Your Home Page

Change the Home Page

1 Display the web page that you want to use as your home page.

2 Click **Safari**.

3 Click **Preferences**.

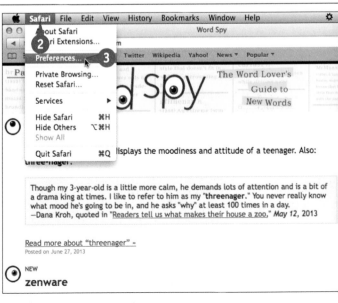

④ Click **General**.

⑤ Click **Set to Current Page**.

Ⓐ Safari inserts the address of the current page in the Homepage text box.

Note: If your Mac is not currently connected to the Internet, you can also type the new home page address manually using the Homepage text box.

⑥ Click ⊙.

View the Home Page

① Click **History**.

② Click **Home**.

Note: You can also display the home page by pressing Shift + ⌘ + H.

Safari displays the home page.

How can I get Safari to open a new window without displaying the home page?

① In the menu bar, click **Safari**.

② Click **Preferences**.

③ Click **General**.

④ Click the **New windows open with** ⟂ and then select **Empty Page** from the pop-up menu.

⑤ Click ⊙.

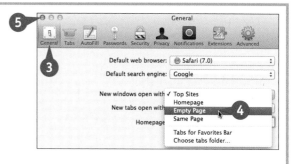

Bookmark Web Pages

If you have web pages that you visit frequently, you can save yourself time by storing those pages as bookmarks — also called favorites — within Safari. This enables you to display the pages with just a couple of mouse clicks.

The bookmark stores the name as well as the address of the page. Most bookmarks are stored on the Safari Bookmarks menu. However, Safari also offers the Favorites bar, which appears just below the address bar. You can put your favorite sites on the Favorites bar for easiest access.

Bookmark Web Pages

Bookmark a Web Page

1. Display the web page you want to save as a bookmark.

2. Click **Bookmarks**.

3. Click **Add Bookmark**.

Ⓐ You can also run the Add Bookmark command by clicking **Share** (⬈) and then clicking **Add Bookmark**.

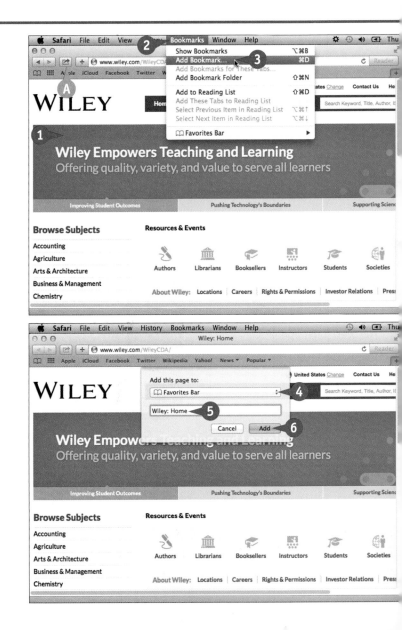

The Add Bookmark dialog appears.

Note: You can also display the Add Bookmark dialog by pressing ⌘+D.

4. Click ⬍ and then click the location where you want to store the bookmark.

5. Edit the page name, if necessary.

6. Click **Add**.

Safari adds a bookmark for the page.

Display a Bookmarked Web Page

1 Click the **Show all bookmarks** button (📖).

B If you added the bookmark to the Favorites bar, click the page name.

C If you added the bookmark to a folder, click the folder and then click the page name.

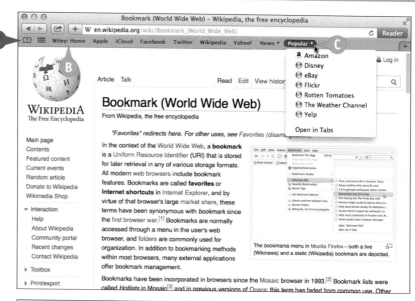

The Bookmarks sidebar appears.

2 Click the location of the bookmark, such as the **Favorites Bar**.

3 Click the folder that contains the bookmark you want to display.

4 Double-click the bookmark.

The web page appears.

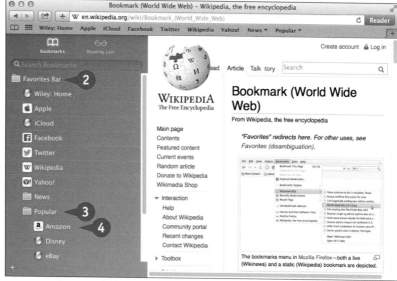

TIPS

I use my Favorites bar a lot. Is there an easier way to display these pages?

Yes. Safari automatically assigns keyboard shortcuts to the first nine bookmarks, counting from left to right and not including folders. For example, you display the left-most bookmark by pressing ⌘+1. Moving to the right, the shortcuts are ⌘+2, ⌘+3, and so on.

How do I delete a bookmark?

If the site is on the Favorites bar, right-click the bookmark and then click **Delete**, or hold down ⌘ and drag it off the bar. For all other bookmarks, click 📖 to display the Bookmarks sidebar. Locate the bookmark you want to remove, right-click the bookmark, and then click **Delete**. You can also click the bookmark and then press Delete.

Search for Sites

If you need information on a specific topic, Safari has a built-in feature that enables you to quickly search the web for sites that have the information you require. The web has a number of sites called *search engines* that enable you to find what you are looking for. By default, Safari uses the Google search site (www.google.com). Simple, one-word searches often return tens of thousands of *hits*, or matching sites. To improve your searching, type multiple search terms that define what you are looking for. To search for a phrase, enclose the words in quotation marks.

Search for Sites

① Click in the Address box.

② Press **Delete** to delete the address.

Ⓐ You can click an item in this list to select the search engine you prefer to use.

③ Type a word, phrase, or question that represents the information you want to find.

Ⓑ If you see the search text you want to use in the list of suggested searches, click the text and skip step 4.

④ Press **Return**.

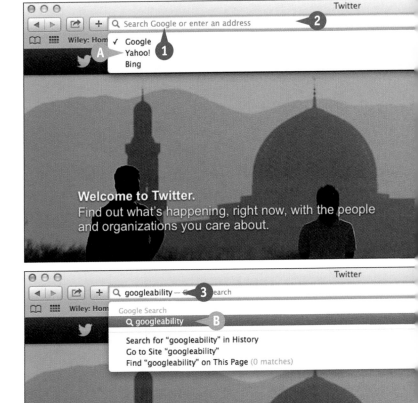

C A list of pages that matches your search text appears.

5 Click a web page.

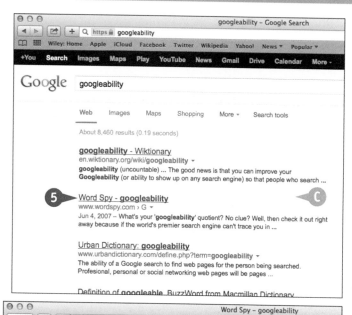

The page appears.

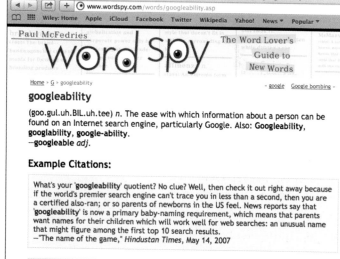

TIP

TIP

Is there an easy way that I can rerun a recent search?
Yes. Follow these steps to quickly rerun your search:

1 Click **History**.

2 Click **Search Results SnapBack**.

You can also press Option + ⌘ + S.

Safari sends the search text to Google again.

Download a File

Some websites make files available for you to open on your Mac. To use these files, you can download them to your Mac using Safari. Saving data from the Internet to your computer is called *downloading*. For certain types of files, Safari may display the content right away instead of letting you download it. This happens for files such as text documents and PDF files. In any case, to use a file from a website, you must have an application designed to work with that particular file type. For example, if the file is an Excel workbook, you need either Excel for the Mac or a compatible program.

Download a File

1 Navigate to the page that contains the link to the file.

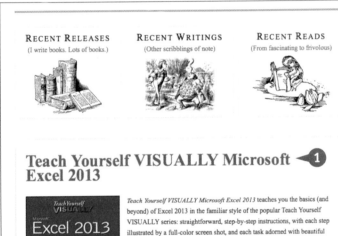

2 Scroll down and click the link to the file.

Safari downloads the file to your Mac.

Ⓐ The Show Downloads button shows the progress of the download.

③ When the download is complete, click the **Show Downloads** button (⦿).

④ Right-click the file.

Ⓑ You can also double-click the icon to the left of the file.

Ⓒ You can click **Show in Finder** (⦿) to view the file in the Downloads folder.

⑤ Click **Open**.

The file opens in Finder (in the case of a compressed ZIP file, as shown here) or in the corresponding application.

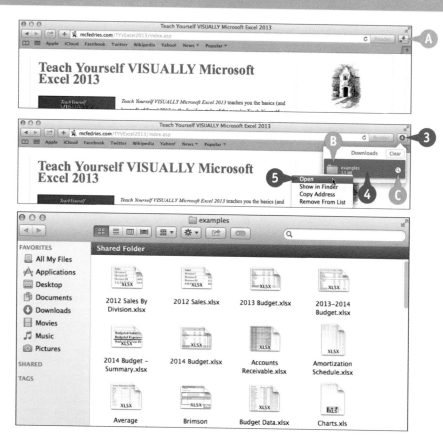

If Safari displays the file instead of downloading it, how do I save the file to my Mac?
Click **File** and then click **Save As**. Type a name for the new file, choose a folder, and then click **Save**.

Is it safe to download files from the web?
Yes, as long as you only download files from sites you trust. If you ever notice that Safari is attempting to download a file without your permission, cancel the download immediately because it is likely the file contains a virus or other malware. If you do not completely trust a file that you have downloaded, use an antivirus program, such as ClamXav at www.clamxav.com, to scan the file before you open it.

View Links Shared On Social Networks

You can make your web surfing more interesting and your social networking more efficient by using Safari to directly access links shared by the people you follow. Social networks are about connecting with people, but a big part of that experience is sharing information, particularly links to interesting, useful, or entertaining web pages. You normally have to log in to the social network to see these links, but if you have used OS X to sign in to your accounts, you can use Safari to directly access links shared by your Twitter and LinkedIn connections. For more information on signing in to your social networking accounts, see Chapter 9.

View Links Shared On Social Networks

1 Click the **Show all bookmarks** button ( ).

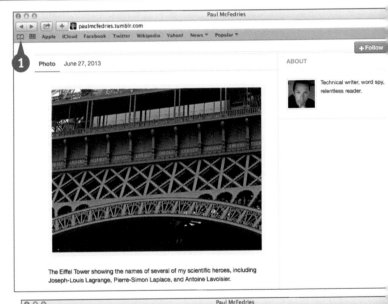

The Bookmarks sidebar appears.

2 Click **Shared Links**.

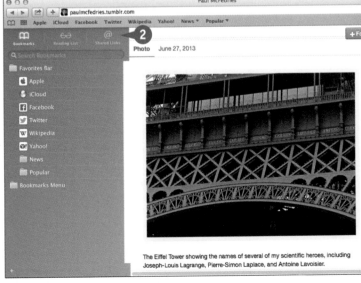

Safari displays the Shared Links sidebar, which lists the most recent links shared by the people you follow on Twitter and LinkedIn.

③ Click the shared link you want to view.

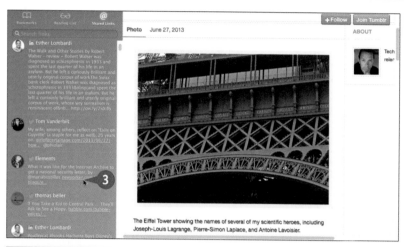

Safari displays the linked web page.

Ⓐ Safari displays the linked web page.

Ⓑ For a Twitter link, if you want to retweet the link to your followers, click **Retweet**.

How can I be sure that I am seeing the most recent shared links?

Safari usually updates the Shared Links list each time you open it. However, to be sure that you are seeing the most recent links shared by people you follow on Twitter or are connected to on LinkedIn, click the **View** menu and then click **Update Shared Links**.

How do I hide the Shared Links sidebar when I do not need it?

To give yourself more horizontal screen area for viewing pages, hide the sidebar by clicking the **Show all bookmarks** button ( ) again. You can also toggle the Shared Links sidebar on and off by pressing Control + ⌘ + 3 .

Create a Web Page Reading List

If you do not have time to read a web page now, you can add the page to your Reading List and then read the page later when you have time. You will often come upon a page with fascinating content that you want to read, but lack the time. You could bookmark the article, but bookmarks are really for pages you want to revisit often, not for those you might only read once. A better solution is to add the page to the Reading List, which is a simple list of pages you save to read later.

Create a Web Page Reading List

Add a Page to the Reading List

1 Navigate to the page you want to read later.

2 Click **Bookmarks**.

3 Click **Add to Reading List**.

Safari adds the page to the Reading List.

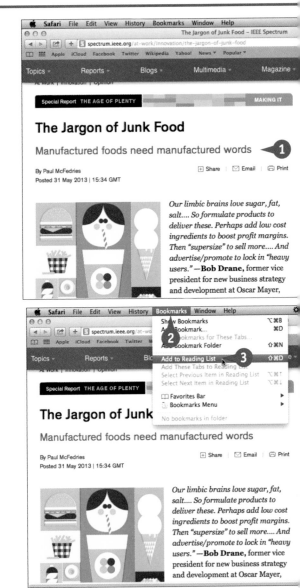

Select a Page from the Reading List

1 Click the **Show all bookmarks** button (📖).

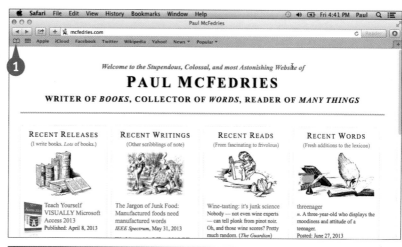

The Bookmarks sidebar appears.

2 Click **Reading List**.

3 Click **Unread**.

Ⓐ If you want to reread a page you have read previously, click **All** instead.

4 Click the page.

Ⓑ Safari displays the page.

CHAPTER 5

Communicating via E-mail

OS X comes with the Apple Mail application that you can use to exchange e-mail messages. After you type your account details into Mail, you can send e-mail to friends, family, colleagues, and even total strangers almost anywhere in the world.

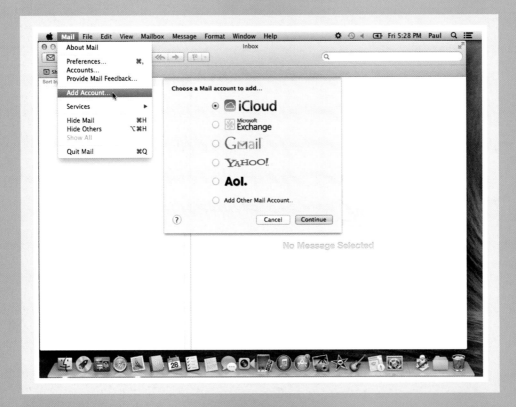

Add an E-mail Account

To send and receive e-mail messages, you must add your e-mail account to the Mail application. Your account is usually a POP (Post Office Protocol) account supplied by your Internet service provider, which should have sent you the account details. You can also use services such as Hotmail and Gmail to set up a web-based e-mail account, which enables you to send and receive messages from any computer. If you have an Apple ID, an account for use on the Apple iCloud service (www. icloud.com), you can also set up Mail with your Apple account details.

Add an E-mail Account

Get Started Adding an Account

1. In the Dock, click the **Mail** icon ( ).
2. Click **Mail**.
3. Click **Add Account**.

Note: If you are just starting Mail and the Welcome to Mail dialog is on-screen, you can skip steps **2** and **3**.

4. Click the type of account you are adding (○ changes to ⊙).
5. Click **Continue**.

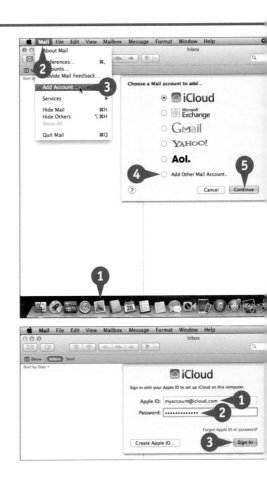

Add an Apple Account

1. Type your Apple account address.
2. Type your Apple account password.
3. Click **Sign In**.

   Mail signs in to your Apple account.

Note: Mail prompts you to choose which services you want to use with iCloud. See Chapter 14 to learn more.

4. Click **Add Account (not shown)**.

   Mail adds your Apple account.

Add a POP Account

1 Type your name.

2 Type your POP account address.

3 Type your POP account password

4 Click **Create**.

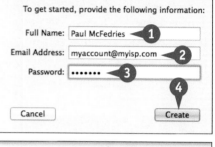

5 Click **POP**.

6 Type the address of the account's incoming mail server.

7 Edit the User Name text as required.

8 Click **Next**.

9 Type the address of the outgoing mail server, which is sometimes called the SMTP server.

10 Type the outgoing mail server username and password, if required by your ISP.

11 Click **Create**.

Note: If you see a Verify Certificate dialog, click **Connect**.

12 Click **Create (not shown)**.

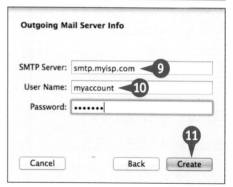

TIP

My e-mail account requires me to use a nonstandard outgoing mail port. How do I set this up?

1 In the menu bar, click **Mail**.

2 Click **Preferences**.

3 Click **Accounts**.

4 In the Outgoing Mail Server (SMTP) list, click ⁑ and then click **Edit SMTP Server List**.

5 Click the outgoing mail server.

6 Click **Advanced**.

7 Click **Use custom port** (○ changes to ●).

8 Type the nonstandard port number.

9 Click **OK**.

10 Click ●.

11 Click **Save**.

Send an E-mail Message

If you know the recipient's e-mail address, you can send a message to that address. An e-mail address is a set of characters that uniquely identifies the location of an Internet mailbox. Each address takes the form *username@domain*, where *username* is the name of the person's account with the ISP or with an organization; and *domain* is the Internet name of the company that provides the person's account. When you send a message, it travels through your ISP's outgoing mail server, which routes the messages to the recipient's incoming mail server, which then stores the message in the recipient's mailbox.

Send an E-mail Message

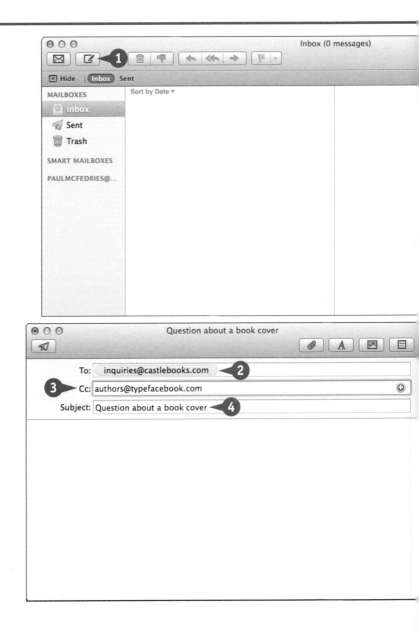

1 Click **New Message** ( ).

Note: You can also start a new message by pressing + .

A message window appears.

2 Type the e-mail address of the person to whom you are sending the message in the To field box.

3 Type the e-mail address of the person to whom you are sending a copy of the message in the Cc field.

Note: You can add multiple e-mail addresses in both the To line and the Cc line by separating each address with a comma (,).

4 Type a brief description of the message in the Subject field.

5 Type the message.

A To change the message font, click **Fonts** (A) to display the Font panel.

B To change the overall look of the message, click **Show Stationery** (▦) and then click a theme.

Note: Many people use e-mail programs that cannot process text formatting. Unless you are sure your recipient's program supports formatting, it is best to send plain-text messages. To do this, click **Format** and then click **Make Plain Text**.

6 Click **Send** (◁).

Mail sends your message.

Note: Mail stores a copy of your message in the Sent folder.

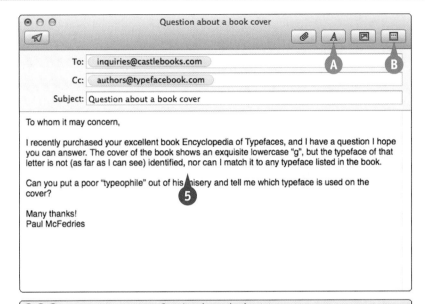

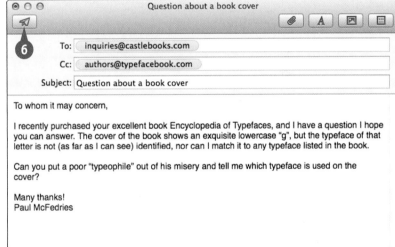

TIP

How can I compose a large number of messages offline?

You can compose your messages offline by following these steps:

1 While disconnected from the Internet, click the **Mail** icon (✉) in the Dock to start Mail.

2 To ensure you are working offline, click **Mailbox**. If the Take All Accounts Offline command is enabled, click that command.

3 Compose and send the message. Each time you click **Send** (◁), your message is stored temporarily in the Outbox folder.

4 When you are done, connect to the Internet.

After a few moments, Mail automatically sends all the messages in the Outbox folder.

Add a File Attachment

If you have a file you want to send to another person, you can attach it to an e-mail message. A typical message is fine for short notes, but you may have something more complex to communicate, such as budget numbers or a slide show, or some form of media that you want to share, such as an image.

These more complex types of data come in a separate file — such as a spreadsheet, presentation file or picture file — so you need to send that file to your recipient. You do this by attaching the file to an e-mail message.

Add a File Attachment

① Click **New Message** (⬚).

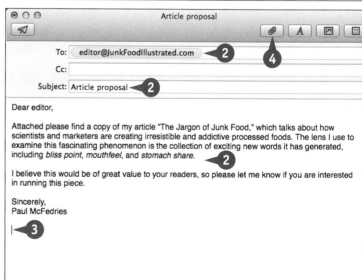

A message window appears.

② Fill in the recipients, subject, and message text as described in the previous section.

③ Press **Return** two or three times to move the cursor a few lines below your message.

④ Click **Attach** (⬚).

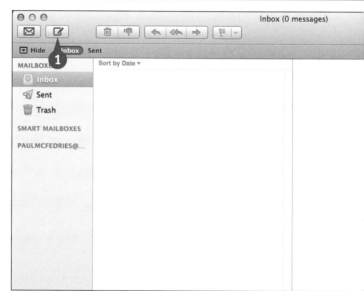

A file selection dialog appears.

⑤ Click the file you want to attach.

⑥ Click **Choose File**.

Ⓐ Mail attaches the file to the message.

Note: Another way to attach a file to a message is to click and drag the file from Finder and drop it inside the message.

⑦ Repeat steps 4 to 6 to attach additional files to the message.

⑧ Click **Send** (✈).

Mail sends your message.

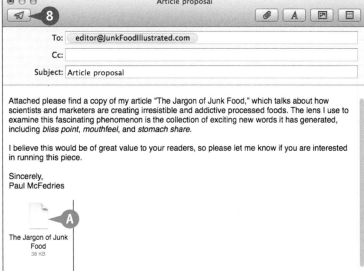

Is there a limit to the number of files I can attach to a message?

The number of files you can attach to the message has no practical limit. However, you should be careful with the total *size* of the files you send to someone. If either of you has a slow Internet connection, then sending or receiving the message can take an extremely long time. Also, many ISPs place a limit on the size of a message's attachments, which is usually between 2MB and 5MB. In general, use e-mail to send only a few small files at a time.

Add a Signature

A *signature* is a small amount of text that appears at the bottom of an e-mail message. Instead of typing this information manually, you can save the signature in your Mail preferences. When you compose a new message, reply to a message, or forward a message, you can click a button to have Mail add the signature to your outgoing message.

Signatures usually contain personal contact information, such as your phone numbers, business address, and e-mail and website addresses. Mail supports multiple signatures, which is useful if you use multiple accounts or for different purposes such as business and personal.

Add a Signature

Create a Signature

1 Click **Mail**.

2 Click **Preferences**.

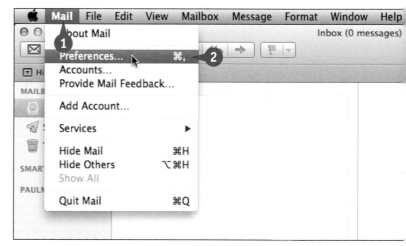

The Mail preferences appear.

3 Click **Signatures**.

4 Click the account for which you want to use the signature.

5 Click **Create a signature** (+).

Mail adds a new signature.

6 Type a name for the signature.

7 Type the signature text.

8 Repeat steps **4** to **7** to add other signatures, if required.

Note: You can add as many signatures as you want. For example, you may want to have one signature for business use and another for personal use.

9 Click ⊝.

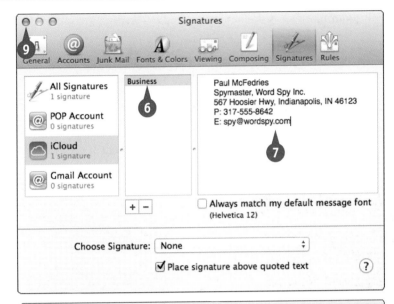

Insert the Signature

1 Click **New Message** (✎) to start a new message.

Note: To start a new message, see the section "Send an E-mail Message."

2 In the message text area, move the insertion point to the location where you want the signature to appear.

3 Click the **Signature** ⬧ and then click the signature you want to insert.

A The signature appears in the message.

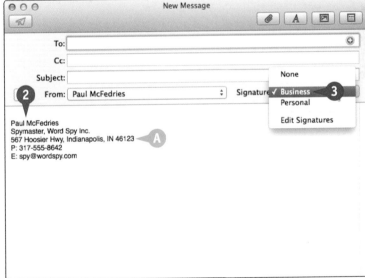

When I have multiple signatures, how can I choose which signature Mail adds automatically?

1 Follow steps **1** to **4** to display the signature preferences and choose an account.

2 Click ⬧ and then click the signature you want to insert automatically into each message.

A If you prefer to add a signature manually, click **None** instead of a signature.

3 Click ⊝.

Receive and Read E-mail Messages

When another person sends you an e-mail, that message ends up in your account mailbox on the incoming mail server maintained by your ISP or e-mail provider. Therefore, you must connect to the incoming mail server to retrieve and read messages sent to you. You can do this using Mail, which takes care of the details behind the scenes. By default, Mail automatically checks for new messages while you are online, but you can also check for new messages at any time.

Receive and Read E-mail Messages

Receive E-mail Messages

1 Click **Get Mail** (⊠).

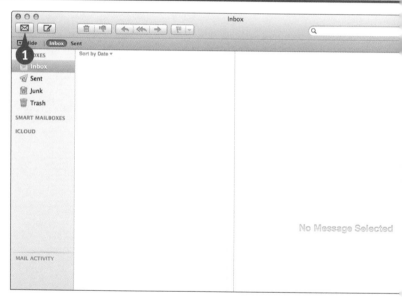

Ⓐ The Mail Activity area lets you know if you have any incoming messages.

Ⓑ If you have new messages, they appear in your Inbox folder with a blue dot in this column.

Ⓒ The 🖂 icon in the Dock shows the number of unread messages in the Inbox folder.

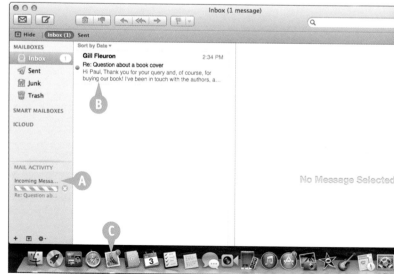

Read a Message

1 Click the message.

Mail displays the message text in the preview pane.

2 Read the message text in the preview pane.

Note: If you want to open the message in its own window, double-click the message.

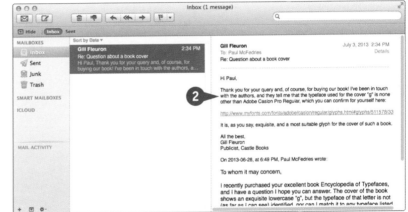

TIP

Can I change how often Mail automatically checks for messages?
Yes, by following these steps:

1 Click **Mail**.

2 Click **Preferences**.

The Mail preferences appear.

3 Click the **General** tab.

4 Click the **Check for new messages** ⁝ and then click the time interval that you want Mail to use when checking for new messages automatically.

If you do not want Mail to check for messages automatically, click **Manually** instead.

5 Click ◯.

Reply to a Message

When a message you receive requires a response — whether it is answering a question, supplying information, or providing comments — you can reply to that message. Most replies go only to the person who sent the original message. However, it is also possible to send the reply to all the people who were included in the original message's To and Cc lines. Mail includes the text of the original message in the reply, but you should edit the original message text to include only enough of the original message to put your reply into context.

Reply to a Message

1 Click the message to which you want to reply.

2 Click the reply type you want to use.

Click **Reply** (⤺) to respond only to the person who sent the message.

Click **Reply All** (⤺) to respond to all the addresses in the message's From, To, and Cc lines.

A message window appears.

Ⓐ Mail automatically inserts the recipient addresses.

Ⓑ Mail also inserts the subject line, preceded by Re:.

Ⓒ Mail includes the original message text at the bottom of the reply.

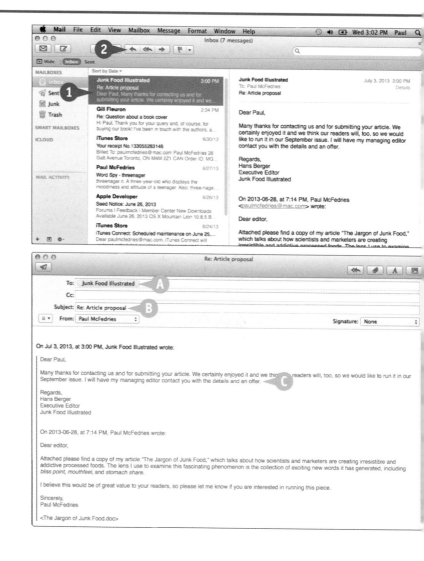

3 Edit the original message to include only the text that is relevant to your reply.

4 Click the area above the original message text and type your reply.

5 Click **Send** (<img>).

Mail sends your reply.

Note: Mail stores a copy of your reply in the Sent folder.

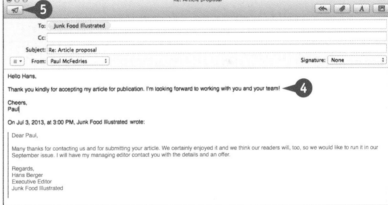

TIP

I received a message inadvertently. Is there a way that I can pass it along to the correct recipient?
Yes. Mail comes with a feature that enables you to pass along inadvertent messages to the correct recipient. Click the message that you received inadvertently, click **Message**, and then click **Redirect** (or press Shift + ⌘ + E). Type the recipient's address and then click **Send**. Replies to this message will be sent to the original sender, not to you.

Forward a Message

If a message has information relevant to or that concerns another person, you can forward a copy of the message to that person. You can also include your own comments in the forward.

In the body of the forward, Mail includes the original message's addresses, date, and subject line. Below this information Mail also includes the text of the original message. In most cases, you will leave the entire message intact so your recipient can see it. However, if only part of the message is relevant to the recipient, you should edit the original message accordingly.

Forward a Message

① Click the message that you want to forward.

② Click **Forward** (➡).

Note: You can also press
Shift + ⌘ + F.

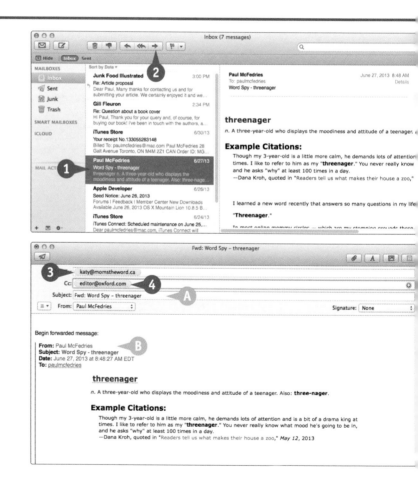

A message window appears.

Ⓐ Mail inserts the subject line, preceded by Fwd:.

Ⓑ The original message's addressees (To and From), date, subject, and text are included at the top of the forward.

③ Type the e-mail address of the person to whom you are forwarding the message.

④ To send a copy of the forward to another person, type that person's e-mail address in the Cc line.

5 Edit the original message to include only the text that is relevant to your forward.

6 Click the area above the original message text and type your comments.

7 Click **Send** (✈).

Mail sends your forward.

Note: Mail stores a copy of your forward in the Sent folder.

Note: You can forward someone a copy of the actual message instead of just a copy of the message text. Click the message, click **Message**, and then click **Forward As Attachment**. Mail creates a new message and includes the original message as an attachment.

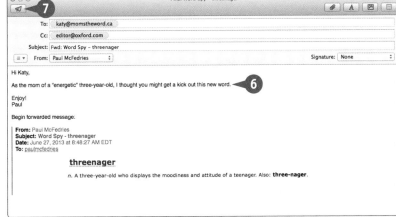

TIP

Mail always formats my replies as rich text, even when the original message is plain text. How can I fix this problem?

You can configure Mail to always reply using the same format as the original message. Follow these steps:

1 Click **Mail**.

2 Click **Preferences**.

The Mail preferences appear.

3 Click the **Composing** tab.

4 Click the **Use the same message format as the original message** check box (☐ changes to ☑).

5 Click **Close** (⊙).

Open and Save an Attachment

If you receive a message that has a file attached, you can open the attachment to view the contents of the file. However, although some attachments only require a quick viewing, other attachments may contain information that you want to keep. In this case, you should save these files to your Mac's hard drive so that you can open them later without having to launch Mail.

Be careful when dealing with attached files. Computer viruses are often transmitted by e-mail attachments.

Open and Save an Attachment

Open an Attachment

1 Click the message that has the attachment, as indicated by the **Attachment** symbol (✐).

A An icon appears for each message attachment.

2 Double-click the attachment you want to open.

The file opens in the associated application.

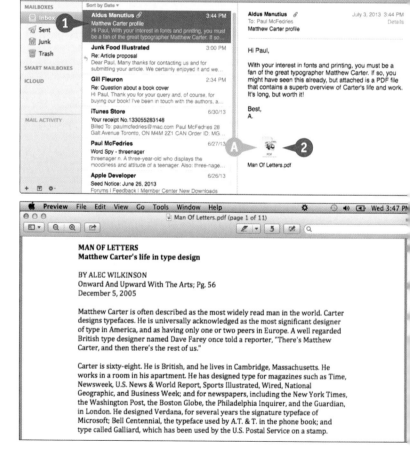

Save an Attachment

1 Click the message that has the attachment, as indicated by the Attachment symbol ( ).

2 Right-click the attachment you want to save.

3 Click **Save Attachment**.

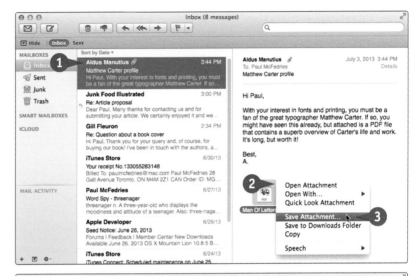

Mail prompts you to save the file.

4 Click in the **Save As** text box and edit the filename, if desired.

5 Click the arrows ( ) and select the folder into which you want the file saved.

6 Click **Save**.

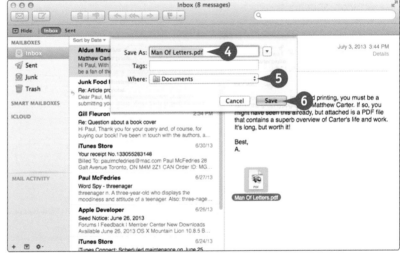

Can I open an attachment using a different application?
In most cases, yes. OS X usually has a default application that it uses when you double-click a file attachment. However, it also usually defines one or more other applications that are capable of opening the file. To check this out, right-click the icon of the attachment you want to open and then click **Open With**. In the menu that appears, click the application that you prefer to use to open the file.

Are viruses a big problem on the Mac?
No, not yet. Most viruses target Windows PCs and only a few malicious programs target the Mac. However, as the Mac becomes more popular, expect to see more Mac-targeted virus programs. Therefore, you should still exercise caution when opening e-mail attachments.

Create a Mailbox for Saving Messages

After you have used Mail for a while, you may find that you have many messages in your Inbox. To keep the Inbox uncluttered, you can create new mailboxes and then move messages from the Inbox to the new mailboxes.

You should use each mailbox you create to save related messages. For example, you could create separate mailboxes for people you correspond with regularly, projects you are working on, different work departments, and so on.

Create a Mailbox for Saving Messages

Create a Mailbox

1 Click **Mailbox**.

2 Click **New Mailbox**.

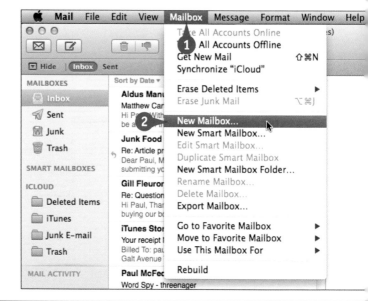

The New Mailbox dialog appears.

3 Click the **Location** ⁝ and then click where you want the mailbox located.

4 Type the name of the new mailbox.

5 Click **OK**.

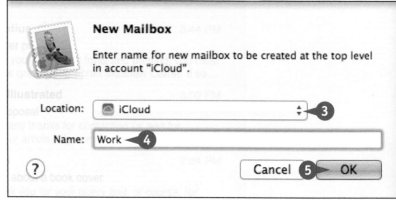

Ⓐ The new mailbox appears in the Mailbox list.

Move a Message to Another Mailbox

1 Position the mouse ▶ over the message you want to move.

2 Click and drag the message and drop it on the mailbox to which you want to move it.

Mail moves the message.

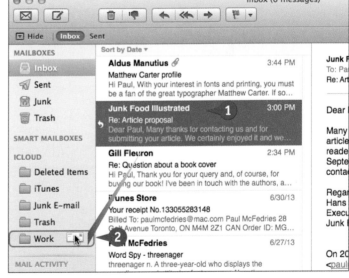

How do I rename a mailbox?

Right-click the mailbox and then click **Rename Mailbox**. Type the new name and then press Return. Note that Mail does not allow you to rename any of the built-in mailboxes, including Inbox, Drafts, and Trash.

How do I delete a mailbox?

Right-click the mailbox and then click **Delete**. When Mail asks you to confirm the deletion, click **Delete**. Note that Mail does not allow you to delete any of the built-in mailboxes, including Inbox, Drafts, and Trash. Remember, too, that when you delete a mailbox, you also delete any messages stored in that mailbox.

CHAPTER 6

Talking via Messages and FaceTime

OS X comes with the Messages application, which you use to exchange instant messages with other OS X users, as well as anyone with an iPhone, iPad, or iPod touch. You can also use FaceTime to make video calls to other people.

Configure Messages

OS X Mavericks includes the Messages application to enable you to use the iMessage technology to exchange instant messages with other people who are online. The first time you open Messages, you must run through a short configuration process to set up your account. This process involves signing in with your Apple ID and deciding whether you want Messages to send out notifications that tell people when you have read the messages they send to you.

Configure Messages

1 Click **Messages** (💬).

The iMessage dialog appears.

2 Type your Apple ID.

3 Type your Apple ID password.

4 Click **Sign In**.

5 Click to deselect the check box beside each phone number and e-mail address that you do not want to use with Messages (☑ changes to ☐).

6 If you want other people to know when you have read their messages, click **Send read receipts** (☐ changes to ☑).

7 Click **Done**.

Messages is now ready to use.

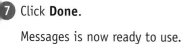

What if I do not have an Apple ID?

You can create a new Apple ID during the configuration process. Follow steps **1** and **2** to open the iMessage dialog, and then click **Create an Apple ID**. In the dialog that appears, type your name, the e-mail address you want to use as your Apple ID, and the password you want to use. You must also choose a secret question and specify your birthday. Click **Create Apple ID** to complete the operation.

Send a Message

In the Messages application, an instant messaging conversation is most often the exchange of text messages between two or more people who are online and available to chat.

An instant messaging conversation begins with one person inviting another person to exchange messages. In Messages, this means sending an initial instant message, and the recipient either accepts or rejects the invitation.

Send a Message

1 Click **Compose new message** (☑).

Note: You can also click **File** and then click **New Message**, or press ⌘+N.

Messages begins a new conversation.

2 In the To field, type the message recipient using one of the following:

The person's e-mail address.

The person's mobile phone number.

The person's name, if that person is in your Contacts list.

Ⓐ You can also click **Add Contact** (⊕) to select a name from your Contacts list.

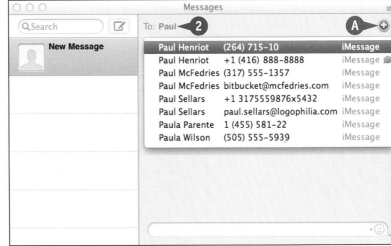

3 Type your message.

B You can also click here if you want to insert a smiley symbol into your message.

4 Press **Return**.

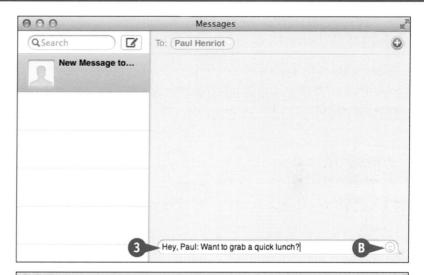

Messages sends the text to the recipient.

C The recipient's response appears in the transcript window.

D You see the ellipsis symbol ( ) when the other person is typing.

5 Repeat steps **3** and **4** to continue the conversation.

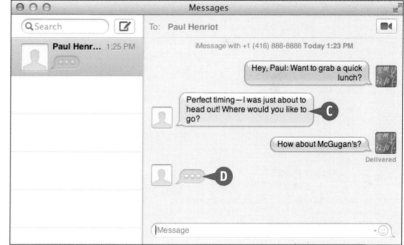

TIP

Can I change my picture?

Yes. Click **Messages** and then click **Change My Picture**. In the Edit Picture dialog that appears, select a category (such as Defaults for the OS X default account images, or Other to choose one of your own images), select the picture, and then click **Done**.

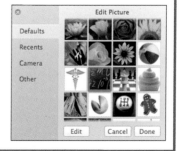

Send a File in a Message

If, during an instant messaging conversation, you realize you need to send someone a file, you can save time by sending the file directly from the Messages application.

When you need to send a file to another person, your first thought might be to attach that file to an e-mail message. However, if you happen to be in the middle of an instant messaging conversation with that person, it is easier and faster to use Messages to send the file.

Send a File in a Message

1 Start the conversation with the person to whom you want to send the file.

2 Click **Buddies**.

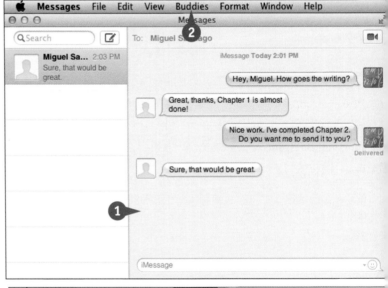

3 Click **Send File**.

Note: You can also press Option + ⌘ + F .

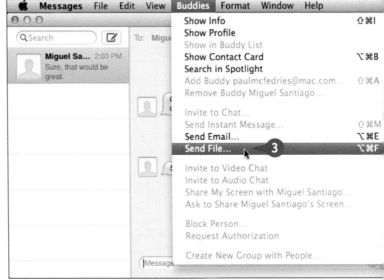

Messages displays a file selection dialog.

④ Click the file you want to send.

⑤ Click **Send**.

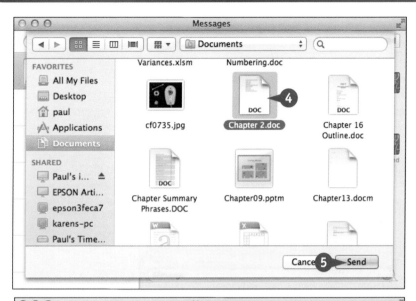

Ⓐ Messages adds an icon for the file to the message box.

⑥ Type your message.

⑦ Press Return.

Messages sends the message and adds the file as an attachment.

TIP

How do I save a file that I receive during a conversation?

When you receive a message that has a file attachment, the message shows the name of the file, with the file's type icon to the left and a downward-pointing arrow (◉) to the right. Click ◉ to save the file to your Downloads folder. Messages saves the file and then displays the Downloads folder.

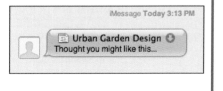

Sign In to FaceTime

FaceTime is a video chat feature that enables you to see and speak to another person over the Internet. To use FaceTime to conduct video chats with your friends, you must each first sign in using your Apple ID. This could be an iCloud account that uses the Apple icloud.com address, or it could be your existing e-mail address.

After you create your Apple ID, you can use it to sign in to FaceTime. Note that you only have to do this once. In subsequent sessions, FaceTime automatically signs you in.

Sign In to FaceTime

1 In the Dock, click
FaceTime ( ).

The FaceTime window appears.

2 Type your Apple ID e-mail address.

3 Type your Apple ID password.

4 Click **Sign In**.

FaceTime prompts you to specify an e-mail address that people can use to contact you via FaceTime.

⑤ If the address you prefer to use is different from your Apple ID, type the address you want to use.

⑥ Click **Next**.

FaceTime verifies your Apple ID and then displays a list of contacts.

What equipment do I and the person I am calling need to use FaceTime?

Your computer must have a web camera, such as the iSight camera that comes with many Macs, and a microphone, such as the built-in microphone that is part of the iSight camera.

Which devices support FaceTime?

You can use FaceTime on any Mac running OS X 10.6.6 or later. For OS X Snow Leopard (10.6.6), FaceTime is available through the App Store for 99 cents. For all later versions of OS X, FaceTime is installed by default. FaceTime is also available as an app that runs on the iPhone 4 and later, the iPad 2 and later, and the iPod touch fourth generation and later.

Connect Through FaceTime

Once you sign in with your Apple ID, you can use the FaceTime application to connect with another person and conduct a video chat. How you connect depends on what device the other person is using for FaceTime. If the person is using a Mac, an iPad, or an iPod touch, you can use whatever e-mail address the person has designated as his or her FaceTime contact address, as described in the previous section. If the person is using an iPhone 4 or later, you can use that person's mobile number to make the connection.

Connect Through FaceTime

1 Click **Contacts**.

2 Click the contact you want to call.

FaceTime displays the contact's data.

3 Click the phone number (for an iPhone) or e-mail address (for a Mac, iPad, or iPod touch) that you want to use to connect to the contact.

FaceTime sends a message to the contact asking if he or she would like a FaceTime connection.

4 The other person must click or tap **Accept** to complete the connection.

FaceTime connects with the other person.

A The other person's video takes up the bulk of the FaceTime screen.

B Your video appears in the picture-in-picture (PiP) window.

Note: You can click and drag the PiP to a different location within the FaceTime window.

5 When you finish your FaceTime call, click **End**.

TIP

Are there easier ways to connect to someone through FaceTime?

Yes, FaceTime offers a couple of methods that you might find faster. If you have connected with a person through FaceTime recently, that person may appear in the FaceTime Recents list. In the FaceTime window, click **Recents** and then click the person you want to contact.

Alternatively, if you connect with someone frequently, you can add that person to the FaceTime Favorites list. Use the Contacts list to click the person, and then click **Add to Favorites**. To connect with a favorite, click **Favorites** and then click the person.

CHAPTER 7

Tracking Contacts and Events

You use the Contacts application to manage your contacts by storing information such as phone numbers, e-mail addresses, street addresses, and much more. You use the Calendar application to enter and track events and to-do items.

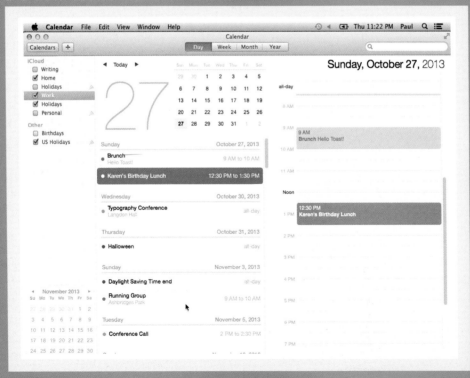

Add a New Contact

O S X includes the Contacts application for managing information about the people you know, whether they are colleagues, friends, or family members. The Contacts app refers to these people as *contacts*, and you store each person's data in an object called a *card*. Each card can store a wide variety of information. For example, you can store a person's name, company name, phone numbers, e-mail address, instant messaging data, street address, notes, and much more. Although you will mostly use Contacts cards to store data about people, you can also use a card to keep information about companies.

Add a New Contact

1 In the Dock, click **Contacts** (📖).

2 Click **File**.

3 Click **New Card**.

A You can also begin a new contact by clicking **Add** (➕) and then clicking **New Contact**.

Note: You can also invoke the New Card command by pressing ⌘+Ⓝ.

B Contacts adds a new card.

4 In the First field, type the contact's first name.

5 In the Last field, type the contact's last name.

6 In the Company field, type the contact's company name.

7 If the contact is a company, click **Company** (☐ changes to ☑).

8 In the first Phone field, click ↕ and then click the category you want to use.

9 Type the phone number.

10 Repeat steps **8** and **9** to enter data in some or all of the other fields.

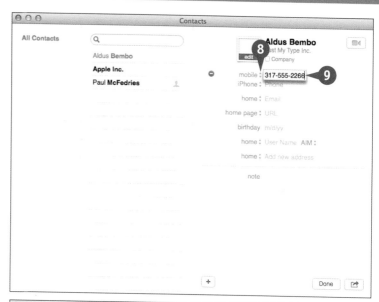

Note: To learn how to add more fields to the card, see the section "Edit a Contact."

11 Click **Done**.

Contacts saves the new card.

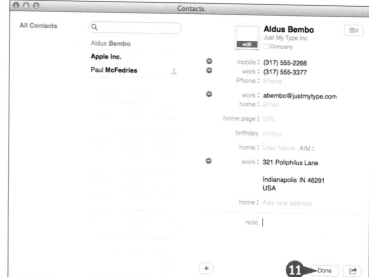

If I include a contact's e-mail address, is there a way to send that person a message without having to type the address?
Yes. You can follow these steps:

1 Click the contact's card.

2 Click the e-mail address category (such as **work** or **home**).

3 Click **Send Email**.

Apple Mail displays a new e-mail message with the contact already added in the To line.

4 Fill in the rest of the message as required.

5 Click **Send**.

Edit a Contact

If you need to make changes to the information already in a contact's card, or if you need to add new information to a card, you can edit the card from within Contacts. The default fields you see in a card are not the only types of data you can store for a contact. Contacts offers a large number of extra fields. These include useful fields such as Middle Name, Nickname, Job Title, Department, URL (web address), and Birthday. You can also add extra fields for common data items such as phone numbers, e-mail addresses, and dates.

Edit a Contact

1 Click the card you want to edit.

2 Click **Edit**.

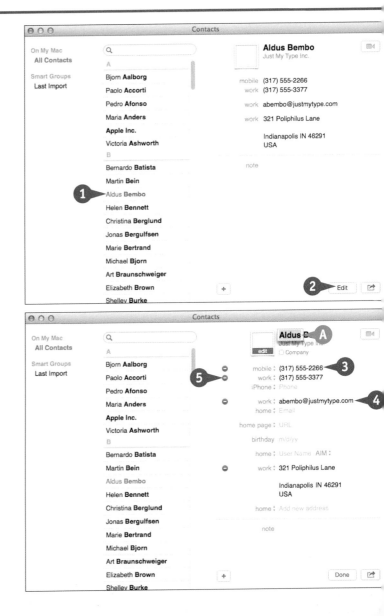

Ⓐ Contacts makes the card's fields available for editing.

3 Edit the existing fields as required.

4 To add a field, click an empty placeholder and then type the field data.

5 To remove a field, click **Delete** (⊖).

6 To add a new field type, click **Card**.

7 Click **Add Field**.

8 Click the type of field you want.

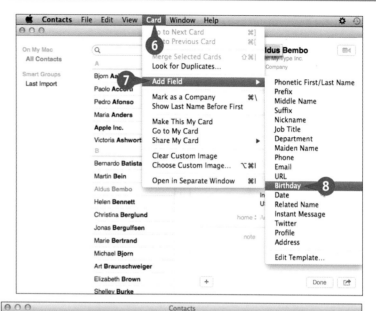

B Contacts adds the field to the card.

9 When you complete your edits, click **Done**.

Contacts saves the edited card.

TIP

How do I add a picture for the new contact?
Follow these steps:

1 Click the contact's card.

2 Click **Edit**.

3 Double-click the picture box.

4 Click the type of picture you want to add.

5 Click the picture.

6 Click **Done**.

7 Click **Done**.

Create a Contact Group

You can organize your contacts into one or more groups, which is useful for viewing just a subset of your contacts. For example, you could create separate groups for friends, family, work colleagues, or business clients. Groups are handy if you have many contacts in your address book. By creating and maintaining groups, you can navigate your contacts more easily. You can also perform groupwide tasks, such as sending a single e-mail message to everyone in the group. You can create a group first and then add members, or you can select members in advance and then create the group.

Create a Contact Group

Create a Contact Group

1. Click **File**.

2. Click **New Group**.

Note: You can also run the New Group command by pressing `Shift` + `⌘` + `N`.

A Contacts adds a new group.

3. Type a name for the group.

4. Press `Return`.

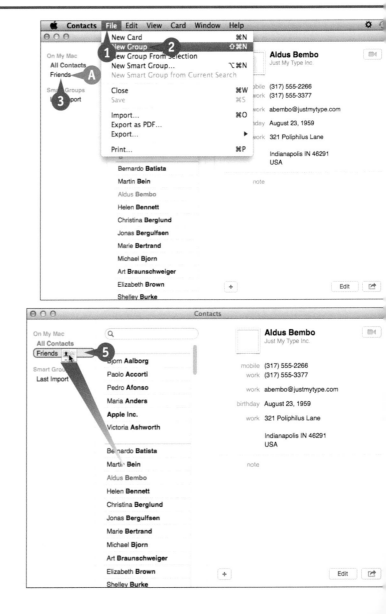

5. Click and drag a contact to the group.

Contacts adds the contact to the group.

6. Repeat step **5** for the other contacts you want to add to the group.

Create a Group of Selected Contacts

1 Select the contacts you want to include in the new group.

Note: To select multiple contacts, press and hold ⌘ and click each card.

2 Click **File**.

3 Click **New Group From Selection**.

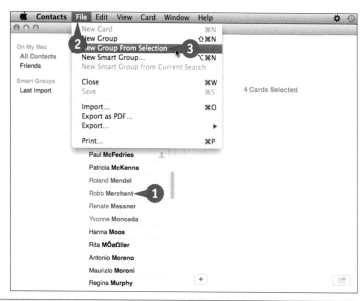

B Contacts adds a new group.

C Contacts adds the selected contacts as group members.

4 Type a name for the group.

5 Press Return.

Can I send an e-mail message to the group?

Yes. With a group, you send a single message to the group, and Mail automatically sends a copy to each member. Right-click the group and then click **Send Email to "*Group*"** where *Group* is the name of the group.

What is a Smart Group?

A *Smart Group* is a special group where each member has one or more fields in common, such as the company name or city. When you create the Smart Group, you specify one or more criteria, and then Contacts automatically adds members to the group if they meet those criteria. To create a Smart Group, click **File**, click **New Smart Group**, and then enter your group criteria.

Navigate the Calendar

Calendar enables you to create and work with events, which are either scheduled appointments or activities such as meetings and lunches, or all-day activities such as birthdays or vacations. Before you create an event, you must first select the date on which the event occurs. You can do this in Calendar by navigating the built-in calendar or by specifying the date that you want.

Calendar also lets you change the calendar view to suit your needs. For example, you can show just a single day's worth of events or a week's worth of events.

Navigate the Calendar

Use the Calendar

1 In the Dock, click **Calendar** (📅).

2 Click **Month**.

3 Click the **Next Month** button (>) until the month of your event appears.

A If you go too far, click the **Previous Month** button (◀) to move back to the month you want.

B To see a specific date, click the day and then click **Day** (or press ⌘+1).

C To see a specific week, click any day within the week and then click **Week** (or press ⌘+2).

D To return to viewing the entire month, click **Month** (or press ⌘+3).

E If you want to return to today's date, click **Today** (or press ⌘+T).

Go to a Specific Date

1 Click **View**.

2 Click **Go to Date**.

Note: You can also select the Go to Date command by pressing **Shift** + **⌘** + **T**.

The Go to date dialog appears.

3 In the Date text box, type the date you want using the format mm/dd/yyyy.

F You can also click the month, day, or year and then click ⏺ to increase or decrease the value.

4 Click **Show**.

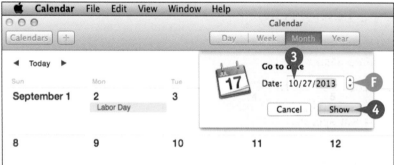

5 Click **Day**.

G Calendar displays the date.

TIP

In the Week view, the week begins on Sunday. How can I change this to Monday?

Calendar's default Week view has Sunday on the left and Saturday on the right. To display the weekend days together, with Monday on the left signaling the start of the week, follow these steps:

1 Click **Calendar** in the menu bar.

2 Click **Preferences**.

3 Click the **General** tab.

4 Click the **Start week on** ⏺ and select **Monday** from the pop-up menu.

5 Click ⏺.

Create an Event

You can help organize your life by using Calendar to record your events — such as appointments, meetings, phone calls, and dates — on the date and time they occur.

If the event has a set time and duration — for example, a meeting or a lunch date — you add the event directly to the calendar as a regular appointment. If the event has no set time — for example, a birthday, anniversary, or multiple-day event such as a convention or vacation — you can create an all-day event.

Create an Event

Create a Regular Event

1. Navigate to the date when the event occurs.

2. Click **Calendars**.

3. Click the calendar you want to use.

4. Double-click the time when the event starts.

Note: If the event is less than or more than an hour, you can also click and drag the mouse (▶) over the full event period.

A. Calendar adds a one-hour event.

5. Type the name of the event.

6. Press **Return**.

Create an All-Day Event

1 Click **Week**.

2 Navigate to the week that includes the date when the event occurs.

3 Click **Calendars**.

4 Click the calendar you want to use.

5 Double-click anywhere inside the event date's all-day section.

Ⓑ Calendar adds a new all-day event.

6 Type the name of the event.

7 Press **Return**.

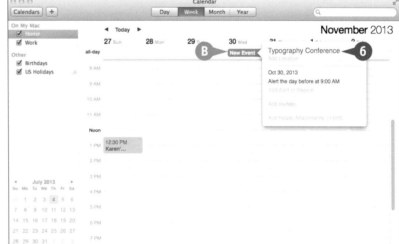

TIP

How can I specify event details such as the location and a reminder message?

1 Follow the steps in this section to create an event.

2 Double-click the event.

3 Type the location of the event in the location text box.

4 Click the event's date or time.

5 Click **Alert** and then click the amount of time before the event that you want to receive the reminder.

6 To add notes, attach a file, or add a Web address, click **Add Notes, Attachments, or URL** and then click the type of information you want to add.

7 Click the event.

Calendar saves the new event configuration.

Create a Repeating Event

I f you have an activity or event that recurs at a regular interval, you can create an event and configure it to repeat in Calendar automatically. This saves you from having to add the future events repeatedly yourself because Calendar adds them for you.

You can repeat an event daily, weekly, monthly, or yearly. For even greater flexibility, you can set up a custom interval. For example, you could have an event repeat every five days, every second Friday, on the first Monday of every month, and so on.

Create a Repeating Event

1 Create an event.

Note: To create an event, follow the steps in the "Create an Event" section.

2 Double-click the event.

Calendar displays information for the event.

3 Click the event's date and time.

Calendar opens the event for editing.

④ Click the **Repeat** ⬆.

⑤ Click the interval you want to use.

Ⓐ If you want to specify a custom interval such as every two weeks or the first Monday of every month, click **Custom** and configure your interval in the dialog that appears.

⑥ Press Return.

Ⓑ Calendar adds the repeating events to the calendar.

TIPS

How do I configure an event to stop after a certain number of occurrences?

Follow steps **1** to **5** to select a recurrence interval. Click the **end** ⬆ and then select **After** from the pop-up menu. Type the number of occurrences you want. Click **Done**.

Can I delete a single occurrence from a recurring series of events?

Yes, you can delete one occurrence from the calendar without affecting the rest of the series. Click the occurrence you want to delete, and then press Delete. Calendar asks whether you want to delete all the occurrences or just the selected occurrence. Click **Delete Only This Event**.

Send or Respond to an Event Invitation

You can include other people in your event by sending them invitations to attend. If you receive an event invitation yourself, you can respond to it to let the person organizing the event know whether you will attend.

If you have an event that requires other people, Calendar has a feature that enables you to send invitations to other people who use a compatible e-mail program. The advantage of this approach is that when other people respond to the invitation, Calendar automatically updates the event. If you receive an event invitation yourself, the e-mail message contains buttons that enable you to respond quickly.

Send or Respond to an Event Invitation

Send an Event Invitation

1 Create an event.

Note: To create an event, see the section "Create an Event."

2 Double-click the event.

3 Click **Add invitees**.

④ Begin typing the name of a person you want to invite.

⑤ Click the person you want to invite.

⑥ Repeat steps **4** and **5** to add more invitees.

⑦ Click **Send** (not shown).

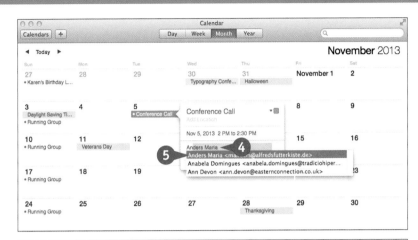

Handle an Event Invitation

ⓐ The Invitation button shows the number of pending invitations you have received via iCloud.

ⓑ The event appears tentatively in your calendar.

① Click the **Invitation** button (⬆).

② Click the button that represents your reply to the invitation:

ⓒ Click **Accept** if you can attend the event.

ⓓ Click **Decline** if you cannot attend the event.

ⓔ Click **Maybe** if you are currently not sure whether you can attend.

TIPS

Is it possible to send a message to all the people who have been invited to an event?

Yes. To send an e-mail message, right-click the event to which you were invited and then click **Email All Invitees**. To send a text message instead, right-click the event and then click **Message All Invitees**.

How do I know when a person has accepted or declined an invitation?

Double-click the event to display its details. In the list of invitees, you see a check mark beside each person who has accepted the invitation; you see a question mark beside each person who has not made a choice or who has selected Maybe; and you see a red Not symbol beside each person who has declined the invitation.

CHAPTER 8

Playing and Organizing Music

You can use iTunes to create a library of music and use that library to play songs, albums, and collections of songs called playlists. You can also listen to music CDs and more.

Understanding the iTunes Library

O S X includes iTunes to enable you to play back and manage various types of audio files. iTunes also includes features for organizing and playing videos, watching movies and TV shows, and organizing apps, but iTunes is mostly concerned with audio-related media and content.

Most of your iTunes time will be spent in the library, so you need to understand the various categories — such as music and audiobooks — that iTunes uses to organize the library's audio content. You also need to know how to configure the library to show only the categories with which you will be working.

The iTunes Library

The iTunes library is where your Mac stores the files that you can play and work with in the iTunes application. Although iTunes has some video components, its focus is on audio features, so most of the library sections are audio-related. These sections enable you to work with music, podcasts, audiobooks, ringtones, and Internet radio.

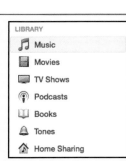

Understanding Library Categories

The Source List button in the upper-left corner of the iTunes window displays the various categories that are available in the iTunes library. The audio-related categories include Music, Podcasts, Books (for audiobooks), Ringtones, and Radio. The Store list includes items you have purchased from the iTunes Store.

Each category shows you the contents of that category and the details for each item. For example, in the Music category, you can see details such as the name of each album and the artist who recorded it.

Configuring the Library

You can configure which categories of the iTunes library appear in the Library list on the left side of the iTunes window. Click **iTunes** and then click **Preferences** to open the iTunes preferences; then click the **General** tab. In the Show section, click the check box for each type of content with which you want to work (☐ changes to ☑), and then click **OK**.

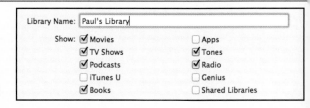

Navigate the iTunes Window

Familiarizing yourself with the various elements of the iTunes window is a good idea so that you can easily navigate and activate elements when you are ready to play audio files, music CDs, or podcasts; import and burn audio CDs; create your own playlists; or listen to Internet radio. In particular, you need to learn the iTunes playback controls, because you will use them to control the playback of almost all music you work with in iTunes.

Ⓐ Playback Controls

These buttons control media playback and enable you to adjust the volume.

Ⓑ Sort Buttons

These buttons sort the contents of the current iTunes category.

Ⓒ Status Area

This area displays information about the item that is currently playing or the action that iTunes is currently performing.

Ⓓ iTunes Store

Click this button to access the iTunes Store, which enables you to purchase songs and albums, subscribe to podcasts, and more.

Ⓔ Contents

The contents of the current iTunes library source appear here.

Play a Song

You use the Music category of the iTunes library to play a song that is stored on your computer. Although iTunes offers several methods to locate the song you want to play, the easiest method is to display the albums you have in your iTunes library, and then open the album that contains the song you want to play. While the song is playing, you can control the volume to suit the music or your current location. If you need to leave the room or take a call, you can pause the song currently playing.

Play a Song

1 Click **Music**.

2 Click **Albums**.

You can also click a sort option such as Songs, Artists, or Genres.

3 Click the album that contains the song you want to play.

Ⓐ If you want to play the entire album, click **Play** (▶).

4 Double-click the song you want to play.

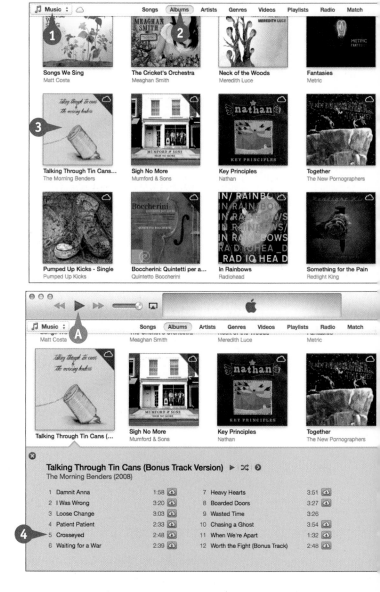

iTunes begins playing the song.

Ⓑ Information about the song playback appears here.

Ⓒ iTunes displays a speaker icon (🔊) beside the currently playing song.

Ⓓ If you need to stop the song temporarily, click the **Pause** button (❚❚).

You can also pause and restart a song by pressing the Spacebar.

Ⓔ You can use the Volume slider to adjust the volume (see the Tip).

Note: See the section "Play a Music CD" to learn more about the playback buttons.

TIP

How do I adjust the volume?

To turn the volume up or down, click and drag the **Volume** slider to the left (to reduce the volume) or to the right (to increase the volume). You can also press ⌘+⬇ to reduce the volume, or ⌘+⬆ to increase the volume. To mute the volume, either drag the **Volume** slider all the way to the left, or press Option+⌘+⬇. To restore the volume, adjust the **Volume** slider or press Option+⌘+⬆.

Play a Music CD

You can play your favorite music CDs in iTunes. If your Mac has an optical drive (that is, a drive capable of reading CDs and DVDs), then you can insert an audio disc in the drive and the CD appears in the Devices section of the iTunes library. When you click the CD, the iTunes contents area displays the individual tracks on the CD, and if you have an Internet connection, you see the name of each track as well as other track data. During playback, you can skip tracks, pause, and resume play.

Play a Music CD

Play a CD

1 Insert a music CD into your Mac's optical drive.

A If you have an Internet connection, after a few moments iTunes shows the contents of the CD.

Note: iTunes shows the contents for most CDs, but it may not show the correct information for some discs, particularly noncommercial mixed CDs.

iTunes asks if you want to import the CD.

2 Click **No**.

Note: To learn how to import a CD, see the section "Import Tracks from a Music CD."

3 Click the **Play** button (▶).

iTunes begins playing the CD from the first track.

Skip a Track

1 Click the **Next** button (▶▶) to skip to the next track.

You can also skip to the next track by pressing ⌘+→.

2 Click the **Previous** button (◀◀) to skip to the beginning of the current track; click ◀◀ again to skip to the previous track.

You can also skip to the previous track by pressing ⌘+← twice.

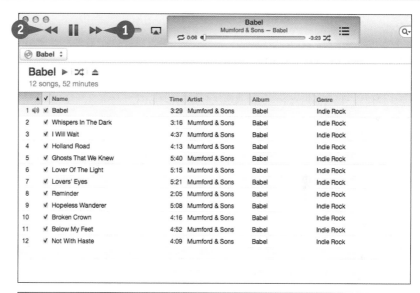

Pause and Resume Play

1 Click the **Pause** button (❚❚) (❚❚ changes to ▶).

iTunes pauses playback.

2 Click the **Play** button (▶).

iTunes resumes playback where you left off.

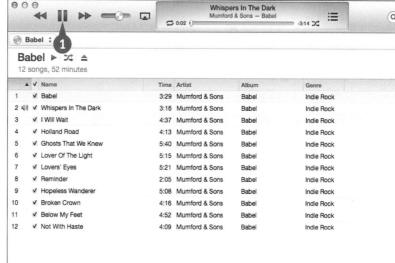

TIPS

Can I change the CD's audio levels?
Yes, iTunes has a graphic equalizer component that you can use to adjust the levels. To display the equalizer, click **Window** and then click **Equalizer** (or press Option+⌘+2). In the Equalizer window, use the sliders to set the audio levels, or click the pop-up menu (⸬) to choose an audio preset.

Can I display visualizations during playback?
Yes. You can click **View** and then click **Show Visualizer** (you can also press ⌘+T). To change the currently displayed visualizer, click **View**, click **Visualizer**, and then click the visualization you want to view.

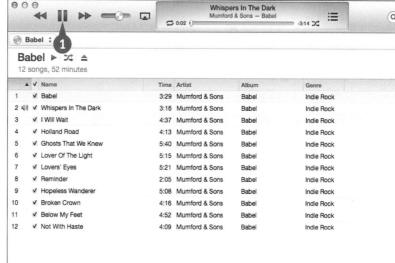

continued ▶

iTunes gives you more options for controlling the CD playback. For example, you can easily switch from one song to another on the CD. You can also use the Repeat feature to tell iTunes to start the CD over from the beginning after it has finished playing the CD. iTunes also offers the Shuffle feature, which tells iTunes to play the CD's tracks in random order. When the CD is done, you can use iTunes to eject it from your Mac. If you want to learn how to import music from the CD to iTunes, see the section "Import Tracks from a Music CD."

Play a Music CD (continued)

Play Another Song

1 In the list of songs, double-click the song you want to play.

iTunes begins playing the song.

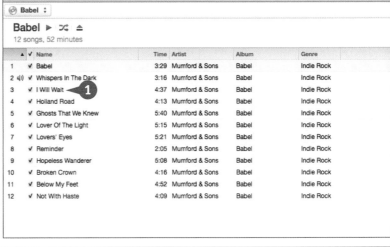

Repeat the CD

1 Click **Controls**.

2 Click **Repeat**.

3 Click **All**.

iTunes restarts the CD after the last track finishes playing.

Ⓐ To repeat just the current song, click **One** instead.

Play Songs Randomly

1 Click **Controls**.

2 Click **Shuffle**.

3 Click **Turn On Shuffle**.

B You can also click the **Shuffle** button (⤨).

iTunes shuffles the order of play.

Eject the CD

1 Click the **Eject** button (⏏) beside the CD.

Note: You can also eject the CD by pressing and holding the ⏏ key on the keyboard.

iTunes ejects the CD from your Mac's optical drive.

TIP

Why do I not see the song titles after I insert my music CD?

When you play a music CD, iTunes tries to gather information about the album from the Internet. If you still see only track numbers, it may be that you do not have an Internet connection established or that you inserted a noncommercial mixed CD. Connect to the Internet, click **Options**, and then click **Get Track Names**.

Import Tracks from a Music CD

If your Mac as an optical drive, you can add tracks from a music CD to the iTunes library. This enables you to listen to an album without having to put the CD into your Mac's optical drive each time. The process of adding tracks from a CD is called *importing,* or *ripping*. After you import the tracks from a music CD, you can play those tracks from the Music category of the iTunes library. You can also use the tracks to create your own playlists and to create your own custom CDs.

Import Tracks from a Music CD

1 Insert a music CD into your Mac's optical drive.

A If you have an Internet connection, after a few moments iTunes shows the contents of the CD.

iTunes asks if you want to import the CD.

2 Click **No**.

B If you want to import the entire CD, click **Yes** and skip the rest of the steps in this section.

3 Click the check box next to each CD track that you do not want to copy (☑ changes to ☐).

4 Click **Import CD**.

The Import Settings dialog appears.

5 Click **OK**.

If you see a dialog asking if iTunes can send CD info to Gracenote, click **Send**.

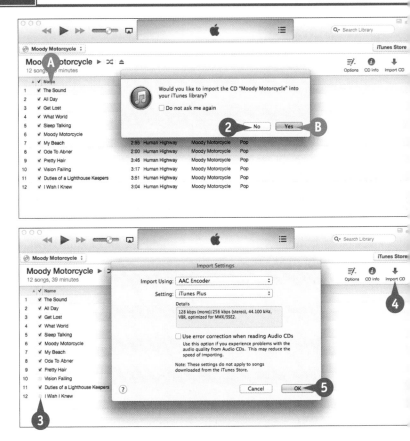

iTunes begins importing the selected track or tracks.

C This area displays the copy progress for each track.

D When iTunes is importing a track, it displays ❄ beside the track number.

E When iTunes finishes importing a track, it displays ✓ beside the track number.

F When iTunes completes the import, you see ✓ beside the track numbers of all the tracks you selected.

6 Click the **Eject** button (⏏) beside the CD, or press ⏏.

TIPS

I ripped a track by accident. How do I remove it from the library?

Click the **Library** button, click **Music**, open the album you imported, right-click the track that you want to remove, and then click **Delete** from the shortcut menu. When iTunes asks you to confirm the deletion, click **Delete Song**. When iTunes asks if you want to keep the file, click **Move to Trash**.

Can I specify a different quality when importing?

Yes, you can by changing the *bit rate*, which is a measure of how much of the CD's original data is copied to your computer. In the Import Settings dialog, click the **Setting** ⁞, click **Custom**, and then use the Stereo Bit Rate pop-up to click the value you want.

Create a Playlist

A *playlist* is a collection of songs that are related in some way. Using your iTunes library, you can create customized playlists that include only the songs that you want to hear. For example, you might want to create a playlist of upbeat or festive songs to play during a party or celebration. Similarly, you might want to create a playlist of your current favorite songs to burn to a CD. Whatever the reason, once you create the playlist you can populate it with songs using a simple drag-and-drop technique.

Create a Playlist

Create the Playlist

1 Click **File**.

2 Click **New**.

3 Click **Playlist**.

Note: You can create a new playlist by pressing ⌘+N.

A iTunes creates a new playlist.

4 Type a name for the new playlist.

5 Press Return.

Add Songs to the Playlist

1. In the Library pop-up, click **Music**.

2. Open an album that has one or more songs you want to add to the playlist.

3. Click a song that you want to add to the playlist.

Note: If you want more than one song from the album's playlist, hold down ⌘ and click each of the songs you want to add.

4. Drag the selected track and drop it on your playlist.

5. Repeat steps **2** to **4** to add more songs to the playlist.

6. Click **Done**.

B. To access your playlists, click **Playlists**.

TIPS

Is there a faster way to create and populate a playlist?

Yes. Press and hold the ⌘ key and then click each song you want to include in your playlist. Click **File**, click **New**, and then click **Playlist from Selection** (you can also press `Shift`+`⌘`+`N`). Type the playlist name and then press `Return`.

Can iTunes add songs to a playlist automatically?

Yes, you can create a *Smart Playlist* where the songs have one or more properties in common, such as the genre or text in the song title. Click **File**, click **New**, and then click **Smart Playlist** (you can also press `Option`+`⌘`+`N`). Use the Smart Playlist dialog to create rules that define which songs appear in the playlist.

Burn Music Files to a CD

If your Mac has a recordable optical drive, you can copy, or *burn*, music files onto a CD. Burning CDs is a great way to create customized CDs that you can listen to on the computer or on any device that plays CDs. You can burn music files from within the iTunes window. The easiest way to do this is to create a playlist of the songs you want to burn to the CD. You then organize the playlist by sorting the tracks in the order you want to hear them.

Burn Music Files to a CD

① Insert a blank CD into your Mac's recordable disc drive.

② If you already have iTunes running and your Mac asks you to choose an action, click **Ignore**.

Ⓐ If you do not yet have iTunes running, use the Action menu to click ⤢, click **Open iTunes**, and then click **OK**.

iTunes displays the instructions for burning a playlist to a CD.

③ Click **OK**.

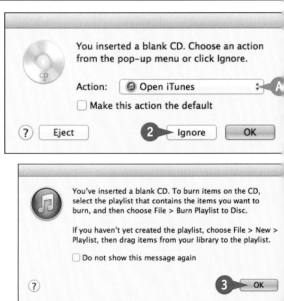

The iTunes window appears.

④ Click **Playlists**.

⑤ Click the playlist that you want to burn.

⑥ To modify the play order, click here.

⑦ Click and drag songs in the order in which you want them to appear on the CD.

134

8 Click **File**.

9 Click **Burn Playlist to Disc**.

The Burn Settings dialog appears.

10 Click **Burn**.

iTunes burns the songs to the CD.

TIPS

Can I control the interval between songs on the CD?
Yes. By default, iTunes adds 2 seconds between each track on the CD. You can change that in the Burn Settings dialog. In the Gap Between Songs pop-up menu, click ⬍, and then click the interval you want to use: None, or any time between 1 second and 5 seconds.

What happens if I have more music than can fit on a single disc?
You can still add all the music you want to burn to the playlist. iTunes fills the first disc and then adds the remaining songs to a second disc. After iTunes finishes burning the first disc, it prompts you to insert the next one.

Edit Song Information

For each song in your library or on a music CD, iTunes maintains a collection of information that includes the song title, artist, album title, genre, and more. If a song's information contains errors or omissions, you can edit the data. For example, it is common for an album to be categorized under the wrong music genre, so you can edit the album to give it the correct genre. You can edit one song at a time, or you can edit multiple songs, such as an entire album or music CD.

Edit Song Information

Edit a Single Song

1 Click the song you want to edit.

2 Click **File**.

3 Click **Get Info**.

Note: You can also press ⌘+Ⅰ. Alternatively, right-click the song and then click **Get Info**.

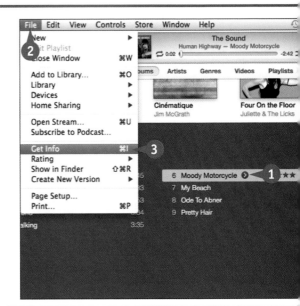

4 Click **Info**.

5 Edit or add information to the fields.

A If you want to edit another song, click **Previous** or **Next** to display the song you want.

6 Click **OK**.

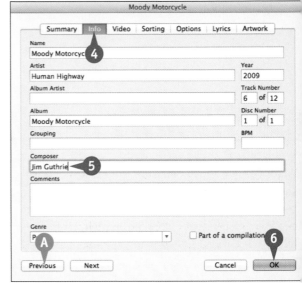

136

dit Multiple Songs

1 Select all the songs that you
want to edit.

ote: To select individual songs,
ress and hold ⌘ and click each
ong; to select all songs (on a music
D, for example), press ⌘+A.

2 Click **File**.

3 Click **Get Info**.

ote: You can also press ⌘+I.
lternatively, right-click any selected
ong and then click **Get Info**.

iTunes asks you to confirm that
you want to edit multiple songs.

4 Click **Yes**.

The Multiple Item Information
dialog appears.

5 Edit or add information to the
fields.

B iTunes displays ☑ beside each
modified field.

6 Click **OK**.

iTunes applies the edits to each
selected song.

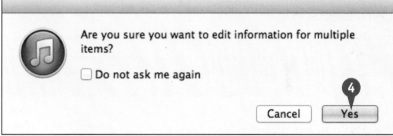

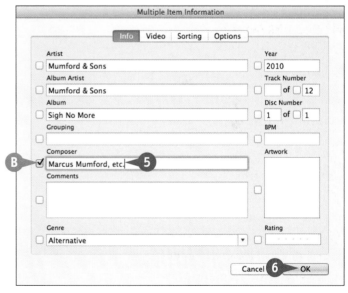

TIP

When I edit multiple songs, why do I not see all the fields in the Multiple Item Information dialog?
When you are editing multiple songs, you can only modify fields containing data that is common to all the
songs, apart from the song title Name field. This makes sense because any changes you make apply to all
the selected songs. For example, each song usually has a different title, so you would not want to give
every song the same title. You see fields that are common to all the selected songs. For example, on a
music CD, data such as the artist, album title, and genre are usually the same for all the songs.

Purchase Music from the iTunes Store

You can add music to your iTunes library by purchasing songs or albums from the iTunes Store. iTunes downloads the song or album to your computer and then adds it to both the Music category and the Purchased playlist. You can then play and manage the song or album just like any other content in the iTunes library. To purchase music from the iTunes Store, you must have an Apple ID, which you can obtain from https://appleid.apple.com. You can also use an AOL account, if you have one.

Purchase Music from the iTunes Store

1 Click **iTunes Store**.

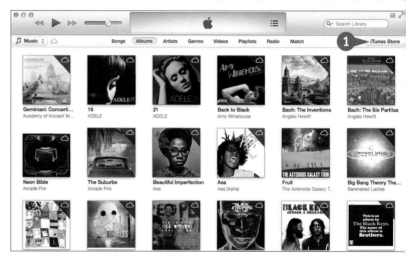

The iTunes Store appears.

2 Click **Music**.

3 Locate the music you want to purchase.

A You can use the Search box to search for an artist, album, or song.

4 Click **Buy**.

B If you want to purchase just a song, click the song's price button instead.

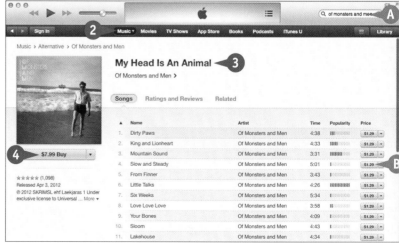

iTunes asks you to sign in to your iTunes Store account.

⑤ If you have not signed in to your account, you must type your Apple ID.

⑥ Type your password.

⑦ Click **Buy**.

iTunes charges your credit card and begins downloading the music to your Mac.

⒞ The status area displays the progress of the download.

⒟ To return to the iTunes library, click **Library**.

Can I use my purchased music on other computers and devices?

Yes. Although many iTunes Store media, particularly movies and TV shows, have digital rights management (DRM) restrictions applied to prevent illegal copying, the songs and albums in the iTunes Store are DRM-free, and so do not have these restrictions. You can play them on multiple devices (such as iPods, iPads, and iPhones), and burn them to multiple CDs.

How do I avoid having many small charges on my credit card bill when purchasing multiple songs?

To avoid many small iTunes charges, purchase an iTunes gift card from an Apple Store or retailer that sells gift cards. On the back of the card, scratch off the sticker that covers the redeem code. Access the iTunes Store, click **Redeem** at the bottom of the store, type the redemption code, and click **Redeem**.

Listen to an Internet Radio Station

The Internet offers a number of radio stations to which you can listen. iTunes maintains a list of many of these online radio stations, so it is often easier to use iTunes to listen to Internet radio. Just like a regular radio station, an Internet radio station broadcasts a constant audio stream, except you access the audio over the Internet instead of over the air. iTunes offers several radio stations in each of its more than two dozen genres, which include Blues, Classic Rock, Classical, Folk, Hip Hop, Jazz, and Pop.

Listen to an Internet Radio Station

1 Click **Radio**.

Note: If you do not see the Radio category, see the first Tip.

iTunes displays a list of radio genres.

2 Click ▶ to open the genre with which you want to work (▶ changes to ▼).

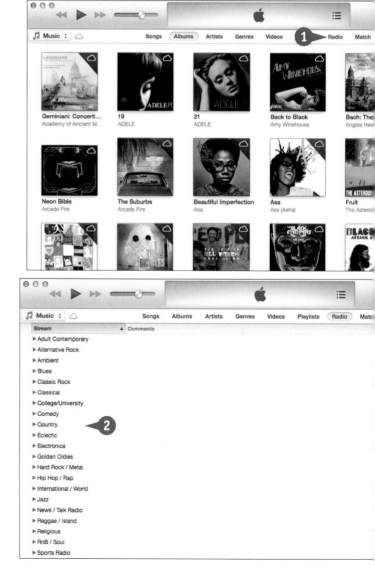

iTunes displays a list of radio station streams in the genre.

③ Click the radio station stream to which you want to listen.

④ Click **Play** (▶).

iTunes plays the radio station stream.

Ⓐ The status area displays the name of the station and the name of the currently playing track.

TIPS

The Radio section of the iTunes library does not appear. Can I still listen to Internet radio?

Yes. By default, iTunes does not show all of the available library categories and sources. To display the Radio source, click **iTunes** and then click **Preferences** to open the iTunes preferences. Click the **General** tab, click **Radio** (☐ changes to ☑), and then click **OK**.

Is it possible to use iTunes to save or record a song from a radio station stream?

No. An Internet radio stream is "listen-only." iTunes does not give you any way to save the stream to your Mac hard drive or to record the stream as it plays.

141

CHAPTER 9

Learning Useful OS X Tasks

OS X Mavericks comes with many tools that help you accomplish everyday tasks. In this chapter, you learn how to synchronize an iPod, iPhone, or iPad; work with notes and reminders; post to Facebook or Twitter; share data; and work with notifications, tags, and maps.

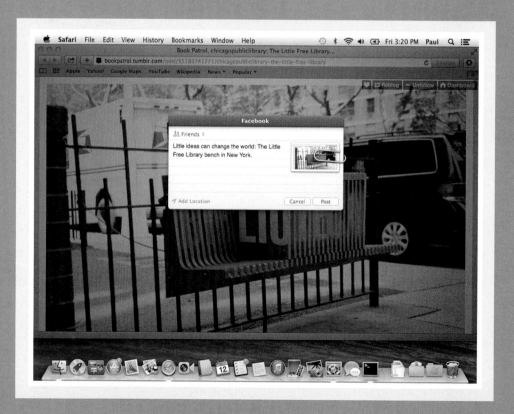

Synchronize an iPod, iPhone, or iPad

You can take your media and other data with you by synchronizing that data from OS X to your iPod touch, iPhone, or iPad. However, you should synchronize movies and TV shows with care. A single half-hour TV episode may be as large as 650MB, and full-length movies can be several gigabytes, so even a modest video collection will consume a lot of storage space on your device. To synchronize you device, first connect it to your Mac and then click the device when it appears in the iTunes menu bar, to the left of the iTunes Store button.

Synchronize an iPod, iPhone, or iPad

Synchronize Music

1. Click **Music**.

2. Click **Sync Music** (☐ changes to ☑).

3. Click **Selected playlists, artists, albums, and genres** (○ changes to ⦿).

4. Click each item you want to synchronize (☐ changes to ☑).

5. Click **Apply**.

6. If you have finished syncing your device, click **Done**.

Synchronize Photos

1. Click **Photos**.

2. Click **Sync Photos from** (☐ changes to ☑).

3. Click **Selected albums, events, and faces, and automatically include** (○ changes to ⦿).

4. Click each item you want to synchronize (☐ changes to ☑).

5. Click **Apply**.

6. If you have finished syncing your device, click **Done**.

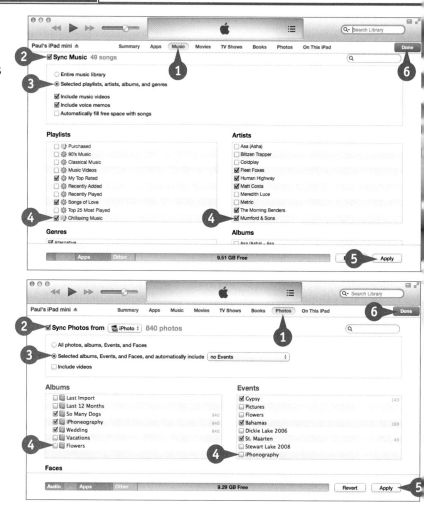

Synchronize Movies

1. Click **Movies**.

2. Click **Sync Movies**
   (☐ changes to ☑).

3. Click each movie you
   want to synchronize
   (☐ changes to ☑).

4. Click **Apply**.

   iTunes synchronizes
   your movies.

5. If you have finished
   syncing your device,
   click **Done**.

Synchronize TV Shows

1. Click **TV Shows**.

2. Click **Sync TV Shows**
   (☐ changes to ☑).

3. Click each TV show you
   want to synchronize
   (☐ changes to ☑).

4. Click **Apply**.

   iTunes synchronizes
   your TV shows.

5. If you have finished
   syncing your device,
   click **Done**.

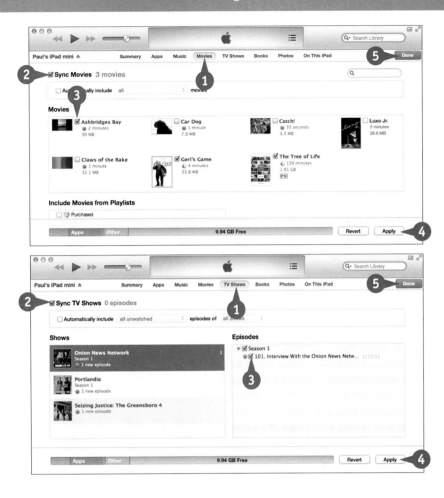

TIPS

Can I sync wirelessly?
Yes. Connect your device and select it in iTunes,
click the **Summary** tab, and then click **Sync with
this *device* over Wi-Fi**, where *device* is iPhone, iPad,
or iPod (☐ changes to ☑). To sync over Wi-Fi, on
your device tap **Settings**, tap **General**, tap **iTunes
Wi-Fi Sync**, and then tap **Sync Now**.

How do I get my photos from my device to my Mac?
You can view and work with device pictures on your
Mac by importing them into iPhoto. In iPhoto, click
your device, then press and hold ⌘ and click each
photo you want to import. Use the Event Name text
box to type a name for this event, and then click
Import Selected.

Install a Program Using the App Store

You can enhance and extend OS X by installing new programs from the App Store. OS X comes with an impressive collection of applications — or *apps* — particularly if your Mac comes with the iLife suite preinstalled. However, OS X does not offer a complete collection of apps. For example, OS X lacks apps in categories such as productivity, personal finance, and business tools. To fill in these gaps, you can use the App Store to locate, purchase, and install new programs, or look for apps that go beyond what the default OS X programs can do.

Install a Program Using the App Store

1 In the Dock, click **App Store** ( ).

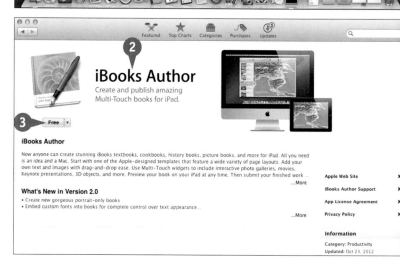

The App Store window appears.

2 Locate the app you want to install.

3 Click the price button or, if the app is free, as shown here, click the **Free** button instead.

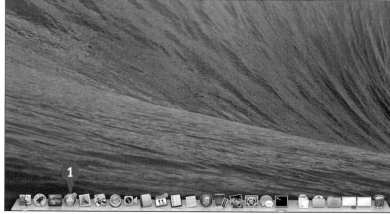

iBooks Author

Now anyone can create stunning iBooks textbooks, cookbooks, history books, picture books, and more for iPad. All you need is an idea and a Mac. Start with one of the Apple-designed templates that feature a wide variety of page layouts. Add your own text and images with drag-and-drop ease. Use Multi-Touch widgets to include interactive photo galleries, movies, Keynote presentations, 3D objects, and more. Preview your book on your iPad at any time. Then submit your finished work ...
...More

What's New in Version 2.0
• Create new gorgeous portrait-only books
• Embed custom fonts into books for complete control over text appearance...
...More

Apple Web Site
iBooks Author Support
App License Agreement
Privacy Policy

Information
Category: Productivity
Updated: Oct 23, 2012

The price button changes to a Buy App button, or the Free button changes to an Install App button.

④ Click **Buy App** (or **Install App**).

The App Store prompts you to log in with your Apple ID.

⑤ Type your Apple ID.

⑥ Type your password.

⑦ Click **Sign In**.

Ⓐ The App Store begins downloading the app.

When the progress meter disappears, your app is installed. Click **Launchpad** (🚀) and then click the app to run it.

How do I use an App Store gift card to purchase apps?

If you have an App Store or iTunes gift card, you can redeem the card to give yourself store credit in the amount shown on the card. Scratch off the sticker on the back to reveal the code. Click 🔵 to open the App Store, click **Featured**, click **Redeem**, type the code, and then click **Redeem**. In the App Store window, the Account item shows your current store credit balance.

Write a Note

You can use the Notes app to create simple text documents for things such as to-do lists and meeting notes. Word processing programs such as Word and Pages are useful for creating comple and lengthy documents. However, these powerful tools feel like overkill when all you want to do is jot down a few notes. For these simpler text tasks, the Notes app that comes with OS X is perfect because it offers a simple interface that keeps all your notes together. As you see in the next section, you can also pin a note to the OS X desktop for easy access.

Write a Note

Create a New Note

1 In the Dock, click **Notes** ( ).

The Notes window appears.

2 Click **New Note** (+).

Note: You can also click **File** and then click **New Note**, or press ⌘+N.

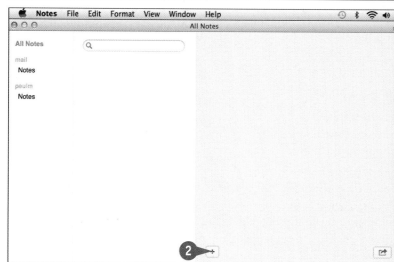

Ⓐ The Notes app creates the new note.

③ Type your note text.

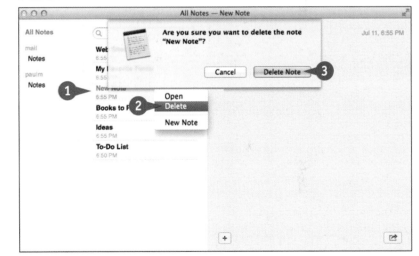

Delete a Note

① Right-click the note you want to delete.

② Click **Delete.**

Notes asks you to confirm.

③ Click **Delete Note.**

The Notes app deletes the note.

Can I synchronize my notes with my iPod touch, iPhone, or iPad?

Yes, as long as you have an iCloud account, you have set up that account in OS X, as described in Chapter 14, and you are syncing notes between your Mac and iCloud. To create a new note using iCloud, click **Notes** under the iCloud folder, and then follow the steps in this section.

How do I create a bulleted or numbered list?

Position the cursor where you want the list to begin, click **Format**, and then click **Lists**. In the menu that appears, click **Insert Bulleted List, Insert Dashed List,** or **Insert Numbered List.**

Pin a Note to the Desktop

You can ensure that you always see the content of a note by pinning that note to the OS X desktop. The Notes app is useful for setting up to-do lists, jotting down things to remember, and creating similar documents that contain text that you need to refer to while you work. Rather than constantly switching back and forth between Notes and your working application, you can pin a note to the desktop, which forces the note to stay visible, even when you switch to another application.

Pin a Note to the Desktop

1 Double-click the note you want to pin.

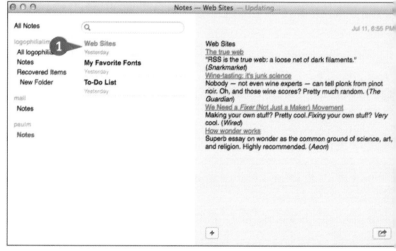

The Notes app opens the note in its own window.

2 Click and drag the note title to the position you want.

3 Click **Window.**

4 Click **Float on Top.**

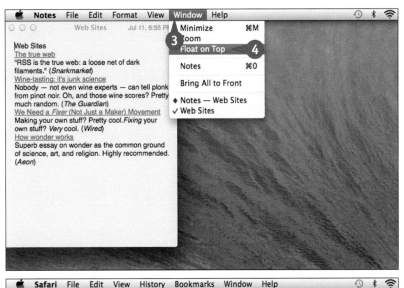

A The Notes app keeps each opened note on top of any other window you open.

Is it possible to pin the Notes app window to the desktop, so that it always remains in view?

No, OS X does not allow you to keep the Notes window on top of other windows on your desktop. The pinning technique in this section applies only to open note windows.

Am I only able to pin one note at a time to the desktop?

No, the Notes app enables you to pin multiple notes to the OS X desktop. This is useful if you have different notes that apply to the same task that you are working on in another application. However, you need to exercise some caution as the pinned notes take up space on the desktop.

Create a Reminder

You can use Reminders to have OS X display a notification when you need to perform a task. You can use Calendar to schedule important events, but you likely have many tasks during the day that cannot be considered full-fledged events: returning a call, taking clothes out of the dryer, turning off the sprinkler. If you need to be reminded to perform such tasks, Calendar is overkill, but OS X offers a better solution: Reminders. You use this app to create reminders, which are notifications that tell you to do something or to be somewhere.

Create a Reminder

1 In the Dock, click **Reminders** (📋).

The Reminders app appears.

2 Click **New Reminder** (✚).

Ⓐ You can also click the next available line in the Reminders list.

Note: You can also click **File** and then click **New Reminder**, or press ⌘+Ⓝ.

③ Type the reminder title.

④ Click the **Show Info** icon ( ).

The Reminders app displays the reminder details.

⑤ Click **On a Day** (changes to).

⑥ Specify the date and time you want to be reminded.

⑦ Click **Done**.

The Reminders app adds the reminder to the list.

Ⓑ When you have completed the reminder, click its check box (changes to).

TIP

What does the At a Location option do?
The At a Location option allows the Reminders app to display a notification for a task when you arrive at or leave a location and you have your Mac notebook with you. To set this up, follow steps 1 to 4, click **At a Location** (changes to), then type the address or choose a contact that has a defined address. Click either **Leaving** or **Arriving** (changes to), and then click **Done**.

Create a New Reminder List

You can organize your reminders and make them easier to locate by creating new reminder lists. By default, Reminders comes with a single list called Reminders. However, if you use reminders frequently, the Reminders list can become cluttered, making it difficult to locate reminders. To solve this problem, you can organize your reminders by creating new lists. For example, you could have one list for personal tasks and another for business tasks. After you create one or more new lists, you can move some or all of your existing reminders to the appropriate lists.

Create a New Reminder List

Create a Reminder List

1 Click **New List** (➕).

Note: You can also click **File** and then click **New List**, or press ⌘+L.

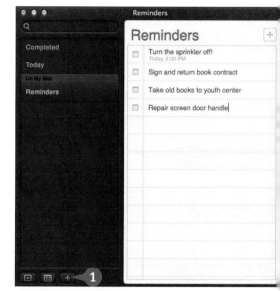

A The Reminders app adds the new list to the sidebar.

2 Type the list name.

3 Press Return.

Move a Reminder to a Different List

① Click the list that contains the reminder you want to move.

② Click and drag the reminder and drop it on the destination list.

③ Click the destination list.

Ⓑ The reminder now appears in the destination list.

Note: You can also right-click the reminder, click **Move to List**, and then click the destination list.

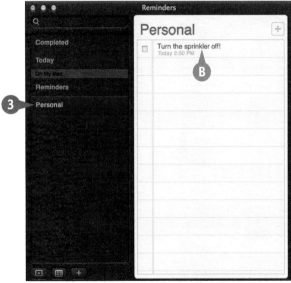

Why does my Reminders app not have a Completed list?

The Reminders app does not show the Completed list when you first start using the program. When you mark a reminder as complete by clicking its check box (☐ changes to ☑), Reminders creates the Completed list and moves the task to that list.

Can I change the order of the lists in the sidebar?

Yes. By default, the Reminders app displays the new lists in the order you create them. To move a list to a new position, click and drag the list up or down in the sidebar. When the horizontal blue bar shows the list to be in the position you want, release the mouse button.

Sign In to Your Facebook Account

If you have a Facebook account, you can use it to share information with your friends directly from your Mac because OS X Mavericks has built-in support for Facebook accounts. This enables you to post status updates and other data directly from many OS X apps. For example, you can send a link to a web page from Safari or post a photo from Photo Booth. OS X also displays notifications when your Facebook friends post to your News Feed. Before you can post or see Facebook notifications, you must sign in to your Facebook account.

Sign In to Your Facebook Account

1 Click **System Preferences** (⚙).

Note: You can also click the **Apple** menu (🍎) and then click **System Preferences**.

The System Preferences window appears.

2 Click **Internet Accounts.**

The Internet Accounts preferences appear.

3 Click **Facebook**.

System Preferences prompts you for your Facebook username and password.

④ Type your Facebook username.

⑤ Type your Facebook password.

⑥ Click **Next**.

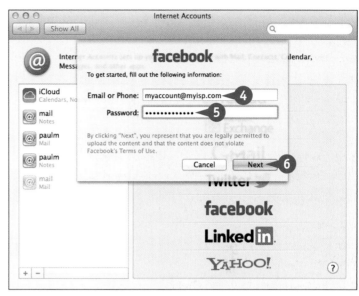

System Preferences displays information detailing what signing in to Facebook entails.

⑦ Click **Sign In**

OS X signs in to your Facebook account.

TIPS

Is there an easy way to add my Facebook friends' profile pictures to the Contacts app?

Yes. Follow steps **1** and **2** to open the Internet Accounts window, click your Facebook account, and then click **Get Profile Photos**. When System Preferences asks you to confirm, click **Update Contacts**.

Can I prevent Facebook friends and events from appearing in the Contacts and Calendar apps?

Yes. Follow steps **1** and **2** to open the Internet Accounts window, then click your Facebook account. If you do not want to clutter Contacts with all your Facebook friends, click **Contacts** (☑ changes to ☐). If you do not want your Facebook events or friends' birthdays to appear in Calendar, click **Calendars** (☑ changes to ☐).

Post to Facebook

Once you sign in to your Facebook account, you begin seeing notifications whenever your friends post to your News Feed. However, OS X Mavericks's Facebook support also enables you to use various OS X apps to post information to your Facebook News Feed. For example, if you surf to a web page that you want to share, you can post a link to that page. You can post a photo to your News Feed

Post to Facebook

Post a Web Page

1 Use Safari to navigate to the web page you want to share.

2 Click **Share** (⬆).

3 Click **Facebook**.

OS X displays the Facebook share sheet.

Ⓐ The web page appears as an attachment inside the post.

4 Type your post text.

5 Click **Post**.

ost a Photo

1 In Finder, open the folder that contains the photo you want to share.

2 Click the photo.

3 Click **Share** (⬚).

4 Click **Facebook**.

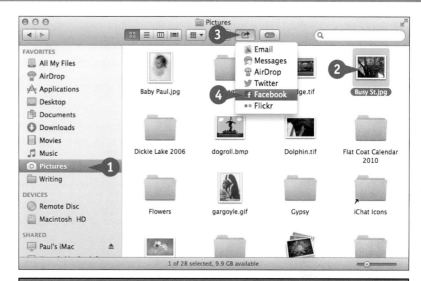

OS X displays the Facebook share sheet.

B The photo appears as an attachment inside the post.

5 Type some text to accompany the photo.

6 Click **Post**.

Can I use OS X Mavericks to post information to my LinkedIn connections?

Yes. OS X Mavericks also comes with support for the LinkedIn social network. To sign in to your LinkedIn account, click **System Preferences** (⚙), click **Internet Accounts**, and then click **LinkedIn**. Type your LinkedIn username and password, click **Next**, and then click **Sign In**.

To share information with your LinkedIn connections, open the app that contains the data, click **Share** (⬚), click **LinkedIn**, type some text to accompany the post, and then click **Send**.

Sign In to Your Twitter Account

If you have a Twitter account, you can use it to share information with your followers directly from OS X Mavericks, which comes with built-in support for Twitter. This enables you to send tweets directly from many OS X apps. For example, you can send a link to a web page from Safari or tweet a photo from Photo Booth. OS X also displays notifications if you are mentioned on Twitter or if a Twitter user sends you a direct message. Before you can tweet or see Twitter notifications, you must sign in to your Twitter account.

Sign In to Your Twitter Account

1 Click **System Preferences** (⬚).

Note: You can also click the **Apple** icon (⬚) and then click **System Preferences**.

The System Preferences window appears.

2 Click **Internet Accounts**.

The Internet Accounts preferences appear.

3 Click **Twitter**.

System Preferences prompts you for your Twitter username and password.

④ Type your Twitter username.

⑤ Type your Twitter password.

⑥ Click **Next**.

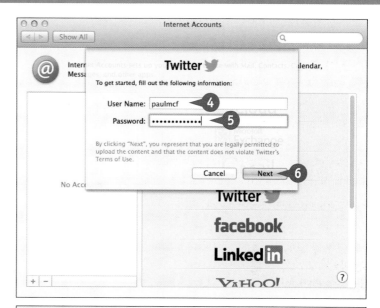

System Preferences displays information detailing what signing in to Twitter entails.

⑦ Click **Sign In**.

OS X signs in to your Twitter account.

TIP

Some of the people in my contacts list are on Twitter. Is there an easy way to add their Twitter usernames to the Contacts app?

Yes, OS X has a feature that enables you to give permission for Twitter to update your contacts. Twitter examines the e-mail addresses in the Contacts app, and if it finds any that match Twitter users, it updates Contacts with each person's username and account photo.

Follow steps **1** and **2** to open the Mail, Contacts & Calendars window, click your Twitter account, and then click **Update Contacts**. When OS X asks you to confirm, click **Update Contacts**.

Send a Tweet

After you sign in to your Twitter account in OS X Mavericks, you can send tweets from various OS X apps. Although signing in to your Twitter account is useful for seeing notifications that tell you about mentions and direct messages, you will mostly use it for sending tweets to your followers. For example, if you come across a web page that you want to share, you can tweet a link to that page. You can also take a picture using Photo Booth and tweet that picture to your followers.

Send a Tweet

Tweet a Web Page

1. Use Safari to navigate to the web page you want to share.

2. Click **Share** (⬈).

3. Click **Twitter**.

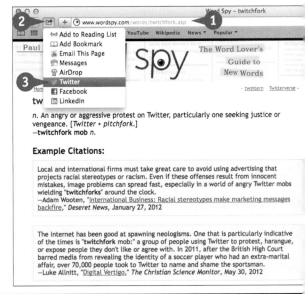

OS X displays the Twitter share sheet.

Ⓐ The attachment appears as a link inside the tweet.

4. Type your tweet text.

Ⓑ This value tells you how many characters you have remaining.

5. Click **Send**.

Tweet a Photo Booth Photo

1 Use Photo Booth to take a picture.

2 Click the picture you want to share.

3 Click **Share** (⬚).

4 Click **Twitter**.

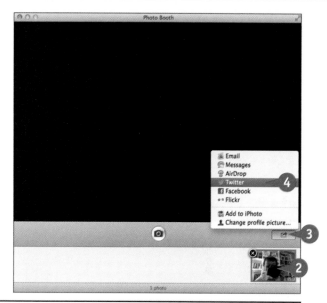

OS X displays the Twitter share sheet.

C The attachment appears as a link inside the tweet.

5 Type your tweet text.

D This value tells you how many characters you have remaining.

6 Click **Send**.

Share Information with Other People

You can use OS X Mavericks to share information with other people, including web pages, notes, pictures, videos, and photos. OS X Mavericks and Mountain Lion were built with sharing in mind. In previous versions of OS X, it was often difficult or tedious to share information such as web pages, images, and videos. OS X Mavericks and Mountain Lion implement a feature called the *share sheet*, which makes it easy to share data using multiple methods, such as e-mail and instant messaging, as well as Facebook and Twitter.

Share Information with Other People

Share a Web Page

1. Use Safari to navigate to the web page you want to share.

2. Click **Share** (⬆).

3. Click the method you want to use to share the web page.

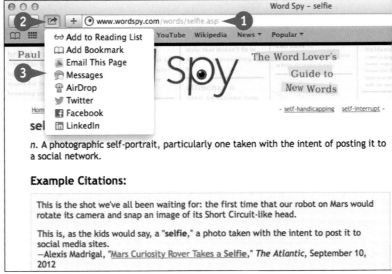

Share a Note

1. In the Notes app, click the note you want to share.

2. Click **Share** (⬆).

3. Click the method you want to use to share the note.

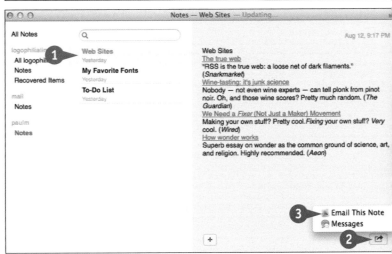

Share an iPhoto Picture

1 In iPhoto, click the picture you want to share.

2 Click **Share** (⬒).

3 Click the method you want to use to share the picture.

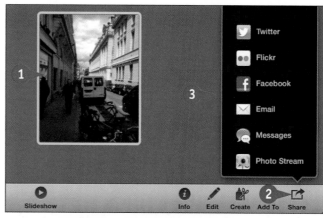

Share a Video

1 In QuickTime Player, open the video you want to share.

2 Click **Share** (⬒).

3 Click the method you want to use to share the video.

Share a Photo Booth Picture

1 Use Photo Booth to snap a photo.

2 Click the photo.

3 Click **Share** (⬒).

4 Click the method you want to use to share the photo.

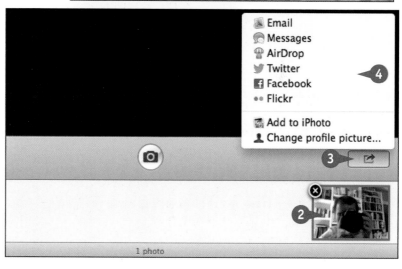

TIP

Do I need to configure OS X to use some of the sharing methods?

Yes. You cannot use the Email method unless you configure Mail with an e-mail account, and you cannot use the Message method until you configure Messages with an account. Flickr and Vimeo must be configured in System Preferences. Click ⬚ in the Dock, click **Internet Accounts**, and then click the type of account you want to add.

Work with the Notification Center

You can keep on top of what is happening while you are using your Mac by taking advantage of the Notification Center. Several apps take advantage of a feature called notifications, which enables them to send messages to OS X about events that are happening on your Mac. For example, the App Store uses the Notification Center to let you know when there are OS X updates available. There are two types of notifications: a banner that appears temporarily and an alert that stays on-screen until you dismiss it. You can also open the Notification Center to view recent notifications.

Work with the Notification Center

Handle Alert Notifications

Ⓐ An alert notification displays one or more buttons.

① Click a button to dismiss the notification.

Note: In a notification about new OS X updates, click **Update** to open the App Store and see the updates. For details about the updates, click **Details**.

Handle Banner Notifications

Ⓑ A banner notification does not display any buttons.

Note: The banner notification stays on-screen for about 5 seconds and then disappears.

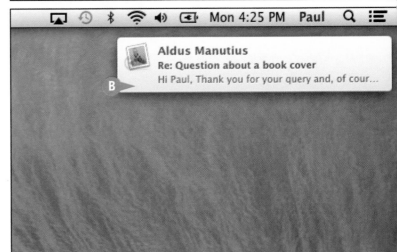

View Recent Notifications

1 Click **Notification Center** (≣).

Note: If your Mac has a trackpad, you can also open the Notification Center by using two fingers to swipe left from the right edge of the trackpad.

C OS X displays your recent notifications.

2 Click a notification to view the item in the original application.

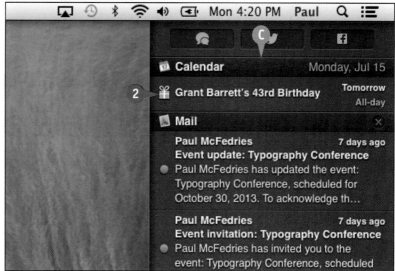

Can I control which apps use the Notification Center and how they use it?

Yes. Click **System Preferences** (⚙) in the Dock and then click **Notifications**. Click an app on the left side of the window, and then click a notification style: None, Banners, or Alerts. To control the number of items the app can display in the Notification Center, click the **Show in Notification Center** option menu and select a number. To remove an app from the Notification Center, click the **Show in Notification Center** check box (☑ changes to ☐).

Organize Files with Tags

You can describe many of your files to OS X Mavericks by adding one or more tags that indicate the content or subject matter of the file. A tag is a word or short phrase that describes some aspect of a file. You can add as many tags as you need. Adding tags to files makes it easier to search and organize your documents.

For an existing file, you can add one or more tags within Finder. If you are working with a new file, you can add tags when you save the file to your Mac's hard drive.

Organize Files with Tags

Add Tags with Finder

1 Click **Finder** (🖐) in the Dock.

2 Open the folder that contains the file you want to tag.

3 Click the file.

4 Click **Edit Tags** (⬭).

OS X displays the Tags sheet.

5 Type the tag.

Note: To assign multiple tags, separate each one with a comma.

6 Press Return.

OS X assigns the tag or tags.

7 Press Return.

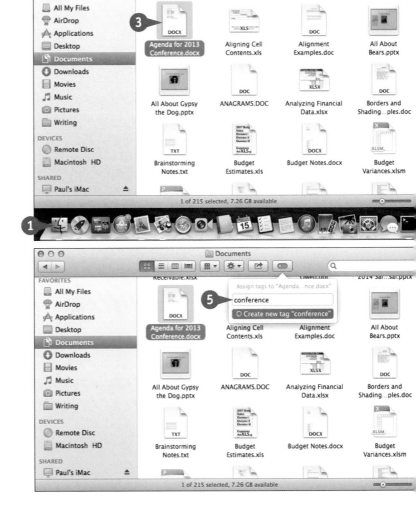

dd Tags When Saving

1 In the application, select the command that saves the new file.

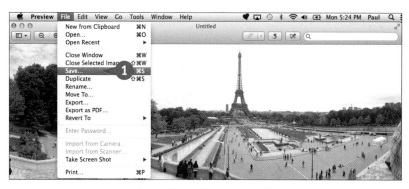

The application displays the Save sheet.

2 Use the Tags text box to type the tag.

ote: To assign multiple tags, eparate each one with a comma.

3 Choose the other save options, such as the filename, as needed.

4 Click **Save**.

The application saves the file and assigns that tag or tags.

Is there an easier method I can use to assign an existing tag to another file?

Yes. OS X keeps a list of your tags, and it displays that list each time you display the Tags sheet. So you can assign the same tag to another file by displaying the Tags sheet and clicking the tag in the list that appears.

Can I assign the same tag or tags to multiple files?

Yes. First, use Finder to select all the files in advance. For example, hold down ⌘ and click each file. Once you select the files, click 🔲 and then type the tag, and OS X automatically assigns the tag to all the selected files.

Search Files with Tags

Once you assign tags to your files, you can take advantage of those tags to make it easier to find and group related files. Although it is good practice to keep related files together in the same folder, that is not always possible. That can make it difficult to locate and work with related files. However, if you assign the same tag or tags to those files, you can use those tags to quickly and easily search for the files. No matter where the files are located, Finder shows them all together in a single window for easy access.

Search Files with Tags

Search for a Tag

① Use Finder's Search box to type the first few letters of the tag.

② When the tag appears, click it.

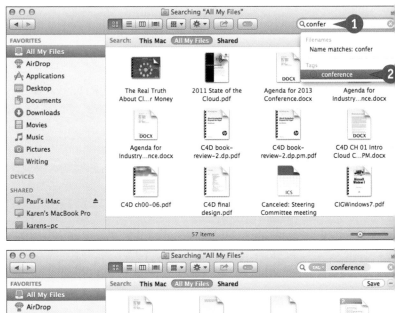

Ⓐ Finder displays the files assigned that tag.

Select a Tag

A In the Finder sidebar, click the tag.

B If you do not see the tag you want, click **All Tags** to display the complete list.

C Finder displays the files assigned that tag.

Note: With the tag folder displayed, you can automatically assign that tag to other files by dragging the files from another Finder window and dropping them within the tag folder.

TIP

Can I control which tags appear in Finder's sidebar?
Yes, by following these steps:

1 Open Finder.

2 Click **Finder**.

3 Click **Preferences**.

4 Click the **Tags** tab.

5 For each tag you do not want to appear in the sidebar, click the check box to the right of the tag (☑ changes to ☐).

6 Click **Close** (⬤).

Search for a Location

You can use the Maps app to display a location on a map. Maps is an OS X app that displays digital maps that you can use to view just about any location by searching for an address or place name. Maps comes with a Search box that enables you to search for locations by address or by name. If Maps finds the place, it zooms in and drops a pin on the digital map to show you the exact location. For many public locations, Maps also offers an info screen that shows you the location's address, phone number, and more.

Search for a Location

1 Click **Maps** ( ).

OS X starts the Maps app.

2 Use the Search box to type the address or name of the location.

Ⓐ If Maps displays the name of the location as you type, click the location.

172

B Maps drops a pin on the location.

C Click **Zoom In** (+) or press ⌘+⊞ to get a closer look.

D Click **Zoom Out** (−) or press ⌘+⊟ to see more of the map.

3 If Maps offers more data about the location, click **Show Info** ( ).

E Maps displays the Info screen for the location.

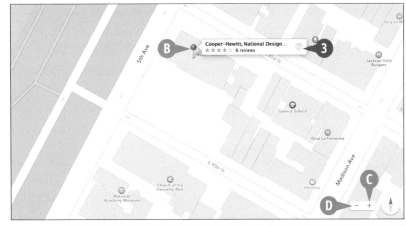

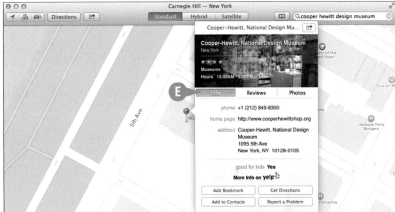

TIPS

Can I use Maps to show my current location?

Yes. Maps can use surrounding electronic infrastructure, particularly nearby wireless networks, to come up with a reasonably accurate calculation of your current location. Click **Current Location** ( ), or click **View** and then click **Go to Current Location** (or press ⌘+L).

How do I save a location for future use?

You can save a location as a bookmark, which saves you from having to type the location's address or name each time. Display the location on the map, click **Show Info** ( ), and then click **Add Bookmark**. You can also click **View** and then click **Add Bookmark**. To see a bookmarked location, click **Show Bookmarks** ( ) and then click the location.

Get Directions to a Location

esesides displaying locations, Maps also understands the roads and highways found in most cities, states, and countries. This means that you can use the Maps app to get specific directions for traveling from one location to another. You specify a starting point and destination for a trip, and Maps then provides you with directions for getting from one point to the other. Maps highlights the trip route on a digital map and also gives you specific details for negotiating each leg of the trip.

Get Directions to a Location

1 Add a pin to the map for your destination.

Note: See the section "Search for a Location" to learn how to add a pin.

2 Click **Directions**.

The Directions pane appears.

Ⓐ Your pinned location appears in the End text box.

Ⓑ Maps assumes you want to start the route from your current location.

3 To start the route from another location, type the name or address in the **Start** text box.

4 Select how you intend to travel to the destination:

Ⓒ Click **Car** (🚗) if you plan to drive.

Ⓓ Click **Walk** (🚶) if plan to walk.

5 Click **Directions**.

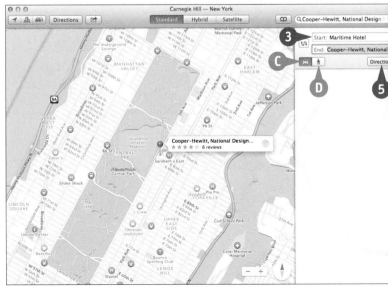

E Maps displays an overview of your journey.

F This area tells the distance and approximate traveling time.

G This area displays the various legs of the journey.

H If Maps displays alternate routes, you can click these banners to view the routes.

5 Click the first leg of the trip.

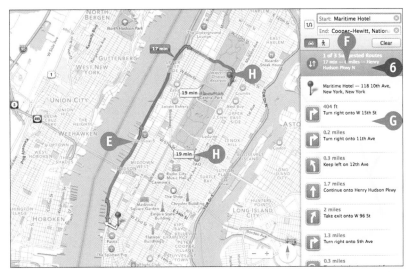

I Maps zooms in to show you just that leg of the trip.

7 As you complete each leg of the trip, click the next leg for further instructions.

TIPS

Can I get traffic information?

Yes, Maps can display current traffic conditions for most major cities. Click **View** and then click **Show Traffic**, or click **Show Traffic** (🚗) in the toolbar. On the map, you see a sequence of red dots where traffic is slow, and a sequence of red dashes where traffic is heavy.

Can I get directions even though I do not have an exact address?

Yes. You can give Maps the approximate location and it will generate the appropriate directions. To specify a location without knowing its address, click **View** and then click **Drop Pin** (or press ⌘+D). Maps drops a purple pin randomly on the map. Click and drag the pin to the location you want.

Install a Font

OS X ships with a large collection of fonts, but if you require a different font for a project, you can download the font files and then install them on your Mac. Macs have always placed special emphasis on typography, so it is no surprise that OS X Mavericks ships with nearly 300 fonts. However, typography is a personal, exacting art form, so your Mac might not have a particular font that would be just right for a newsletter, greeting card, or similar project. In that case, you can download the font you need and then install it.

Install a Font

1 Click **Spotlight** (Q).

2 Type **font**.

3 Click **Font Book**.

You can also open Finder, click **Applications**, and then click **Font Book** (🖌).

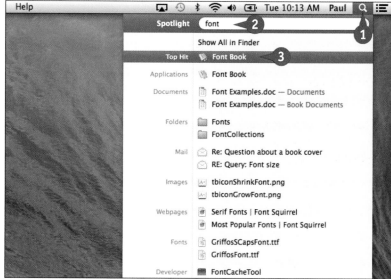

The Font Book application appears.

4 Click **File**.

5 Click **Add Fonts**.

Ⓐ You can also click **Add fonts** (➕) or press ⌘+Ⓞ.

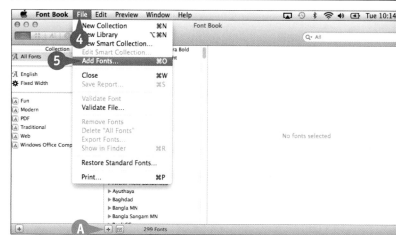

⑤ Open the location that contains the font you want to install.

⑦ Click the folder that contains the font files.

⑧ Click **Open**.

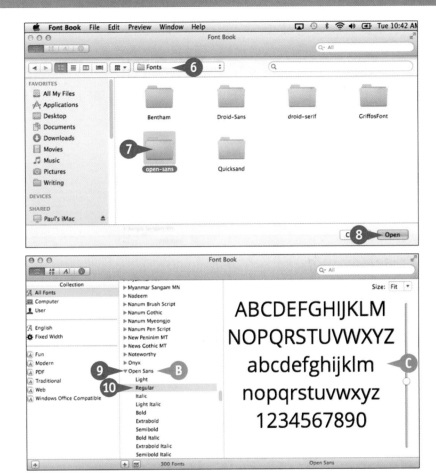

OS X installs the font.

Ⓑ The typeface name appears in the Fonts list.

⑨ Click ▶ to open the typeface and see its individual fonts.

⑩ Click a font.

Ⓒ A preview of the font appears here.

TIPS

What is the difference between a font and a typeface?

A *typeface* is a unique design applied to each letter, number, and symbol. A *font* is a particular style of a typeface, such as regular, bold, or italic. However, in everyday parlance, most people use the terms typeface and font interchangeably.

What is a font collection?

A *collection* is a group of related fonts. For example, the Fun collection contains fonts that are normally used with informal designs, while the Web collection contains fonts that render well on web pages. To add your new font to an existing collection, drag it from the **Fonts** list and drop it on the collection. To create your own collection, click **File** and then click **New Collection** (or press ⌘+Ⓝ).

CHAPTER 10

Viewing and Editing Photos

Whether you just want to look at your photos, or you want to edit them to crop out unneeded portions or fix problems, OS X comes with a number of useful tools for viewing and editing photos.

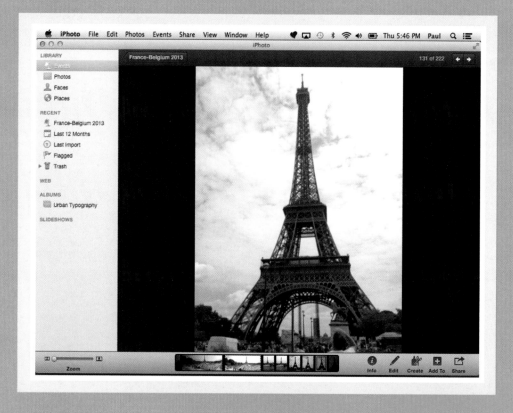

View a Preview of a Photo

OS X offers several tools you can use to see a preview of any photo on your Mac. The Finder application has a number of methods you can use to view your photos, but here you learn about the two easiest methods. First, you can preview any saved image file using the OS X Quick Look feature; second, you can see photo previews by switching to the Cover Flow view. You can also preview photos using the Preview application.

View a Preview of a Photo

View a Preview with Quick Look

1. Click **Finder** (🙂) in the Dock.

2. Open the folder that contains the photo you want to preview.

3. Click the photo.

4. Press Spacebar.

Ⓐ Finder displays a preview of the photo.

View a Preview with Cover Flow

1. Click **Finder** (🙂) in the Dock.

2. Open the folder that contains the photo you want to preview.

3. Click the photo.

4. Click **Cover Flow** (>).

Ⓑ Finder displays a preview of the photo.

iew a Preview in the review Application

1. Click **Finder** (🖳) in the Dock.

2. Open the folder that contains the photo you want to preview.

3. Click the photo.

4. Click **File**.

5. Click **Open With**.

6. Click **Preview**.

ote: In many cases, you can also imply double-click the photo to pen it in the Preview application.

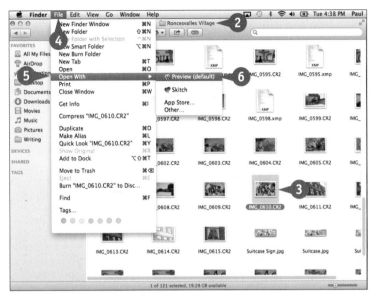

The Preview application opens and displays the photo.

7. Use the toolbar buttons to change how the photo appears in the Preview window.

C. More commands are available on the **View** menu.

8. When you finish viewing the photo, click **Close** (⬤).

Is there an easier way to preview multiple photos using the Preview application?

Yes. In Finder, navigate to the folder that contains the photos, and then select each file that you want to preview. Either click and drag the mouse (🢒) over the photos or press and hold ⌘ and click each one. In Preview, click **Next** and **Previous** to navigate the photos.

Is there a way that I can zoom in on just a portion of a photo?

Yes. In Preview, click and drag your mouse (🢒) to select the portion of the photo that you want to magnify. Click **View** and then click **Zoom to Selection** (or press ⌘+⭐).

View a Slide Show of Your Photos

Instead of viewing your photos one at a time, you can easily view multiple photos by running them in a slide show. You can run the slide show using the Preview application or Quick Look. The slide show displays each photo for a few seconds, and then Preview automatically displays the next photo. Quick Look also offers several on-screen controls that you can use to control the slide show playback. You can also configure Quick Look to display the images full screen.

View a Slide Show of Your Photos

1 Click **Finder** ( ) in the Dock.

2 Open the folder that contains the photos you want to view in the slide show.

3 Select the photos you want to view.

4 Click **File**.

5 Click **Open With**.

6 Click **Preview**.

The Preview window appears.

7 Click **View**.

8 Click **Slideshow**.

You can also select Slideshow by pressing Shift + ⌘ + F.

Preview opens the slide show window.

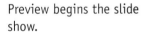 Move the mouse (🡔).

Ⓐ Preview displays the slide show controls.

⓪ Click **Play**.

Preview begins the slide show.

Ⓑ Click **Next** to move to the next photo.

Ⓒ Click **Back** to move to the previous photo.

Ⓓ Click **Pause** to suspend the slide show.

⓫ When the slide show is over or when you want to return to Finder, click **Close** or press Esc.

TIPS

Can I jump to a specific photo during the slide show?

Yes. With the slide show running, press Spacebar to stop the show. Use the arrow keys to select the photo that you want to view in the slide show. Click **Play** to resume the slide show.

What keyboard shortcuts can I use when viewing a slide show?

Press ➡ or 🡑 to display the next photo, and press ⬅ or 🡓 to display the previous photo. Press Esc to end the slide show.

Import Photos from a Digital Camera

You can import photos from a digital camera and save them on your Mac. If you have the iLife suite installed on your Mac, you can use the iPhoto application to handle importing photos. iPhoto is also available separately through the App Store. iPhoto enables you to add a name and a description to each import, which helps you to find your photos after the import is complete. To perform the import, you need a cable to connect your digital camera to your Mac. Most digital cameras come with a USB cable.

Import Photos from a Digital Camera

Import Photos from a Digital Camera

1. Connect one end of the cable to the digital camera.

2. Connect the other end of the cable to a free USB port on your Mac.

3. Turn the camera on and put it in either playback or computer mode.

   Your Mac launches the iPhoto application.

Note: You can also launch the application by clicking **iPhoto** ( ) in the Dock.

Ⓐ Your digital camera appears in the Devices section.

Ⓑ iPhoto displays previews of the camera's photos.

4. Use the Event Name text box to type a name for the group of photos you are going to import.

5 Click and drag the mouse (🔺) around the photos you want, or press and hold ⌘ and click each photo you want to select.

6 Click **Import Selected**.

C To import all the photos from the digital camera, click **Import X Photos**, where *X* is the number of photos stored in the camera.

iPhoto imports the photos from the digital camera.

iPhoto asks if you want to delete the original photos from the digital camera.

7 If you no longer need the photos on the camera, click **Delete Photos**.

D To keep the photos on the camera, click **Keep Photos**.

View the Imported Photos

1 Click **Events**.

2 Double-click the event name that you specified in step 4.

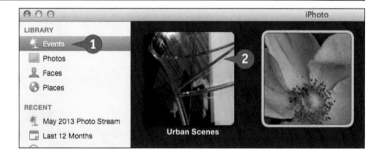

TIP

When I connect my digital camera, why do I see Image Capture instead of iPhoto?
Your Image Capture is not configured to open iPhoto when you connect your camera. You need do the following:

1 Connect your digital camera to your Mac and the Image Capture application opens.

Note: If you do not see the Image Capture application, click **Finder** (🖼️) in the Dock, click **Applications**, and then double-click **Image Capture**.

2 Click the **Connecting** ⁑ and then click **iPhoto**.

3 Click **Image Capture** in the menu bar.

4 Click **Quit Image Capture**.

View Your Photos

If you want to look at several photos, you can use the iPhoto application, which is available with the Apple iLife suite or separately via the App Store. iPhoto offers a feature called full-screen mode, which hides everything else and displays your photos using the entire screen. Once you activate full-screen mode, iPhoto offers several on-screen controls that you can use to navigate backward and forward through the photos. Full-screen mode also shows thumbnail images of each photo, so you can quickly jump to any photo you want to view.

View Your Photos

1 In iPhoto, click **Events**.

2 Double-click the event that contains the photos you want to view.

3 Double-click the first photo you want to view.

iPhoto displays the photo.

③ Click **Next** (⬛) to view the next photo in the event.

Ⓐ You can also click **Previous** (⬛) to see the previous photo in the event.

Note: You can also navigate photos by pressing ➡ and ⬅.

⑤ When you are done, click the name of the event.

TIP

Is there a way that I can jump quickly to a particular photo in full-screen mode?
Yes. Follow these steps:

① Move the mouse (▶) to the thumbnails at the bottom of the iPhoto window.

② Use the horizontal scroll bar to bring the thumbnail of the photo you want into view.

③ Click the photo's thumbnail.

iPhoto displays the photo in full-screen mode.

Create an Album

You can use iPhoto to organize your photos into albums. You can get iPhoto either via the iLife suite, which is installed on all new Macs, or via the App Store. In iPhoto, an *album* is a collectio of photos that are usually related in some way. For example, you might create an album for a series of vacation photos, for photos taken at a party or other special event, or for photos that include a particular person, pet, or place. Using your iPhoto library, you can create customized albums that include only the photos that you want to view.

Create an Album

Create the Album

1 Click **File**.

2 Click **New Album**.

Note: You can also start a new album by pressing ⌘+N.

3 Type a name for the new album.

4 Press Return.

Add Photos to the Album

1 Click **Photos**.

2 Click ▶ beside an event that contains photos with which you want to work (▶ changes to ▼).

3 Click and drag a photo and drop it on the new album.

4 Repeat steps **2** and **3** to add other photos to the album.

5 Click the album.

Ⓐ iPhoto displays the photos you added to the album.

Is there any way to make iPhoto add photos to an album automatically?
Yes, you can create a *Smart Album* where the photos that appear in the album have one or more properties in common, such as the description, rating, date, or text in the photo title. Click **File** and then click **New Smart Album** (you can also press Option+⌘+N). Use the Smart Album dialog to create one or more rules that define which photos you want to appear in the album.

Crop a Photo

If you have a photo containing elements that you do not want to see, you can often cut out those elements. This is called *cropping*, and you can do this with iPhoto, which comes with iLife or via the App Store. When you crop a photo, you specify a rectangular area of the photo that you want to keep. iPhoto discards everything outside of the rectangle. Cropping is a useful skill because it can help give focus to the true subject of a photo. Cropping is also useful for removing extraneous elements that appear near the edges of a photo.

Crop a Photo

1 Click the photo you want to crop.

2 Click **Edit**.

iPhoto displays its editing tools.

3 Click **Crop**.

iPhoto displays a cropping rectangle on the photo.

④ Click and drag a corner or side to define the area you want to keep.

Note: Remember that iPhoto keeps the area inside the rectangle.

⑤ Click **Done**.

iPhoto saves the cropped photo.

⑥ Click **Edit**.

iPhoto exits edit mode.

Is there a quick way to crop a photo to a certain size?
Yes, iPhoto enables you to specify either a specific size, such as 640 × 480, or a specific ratio, such as 4 × 3 or 16 × 9.

① Follow steps **1** to **3** to display the Crop tool.

② Click the **Constrain** check box (☐ changes to ☑).

③ In the Constrain pop-up menu, click ↕.

④ Click the size or ratio you want to use.

⑤ Click **Done**.

⑥ Click **Edit**.

iPhoto exits edit mode.

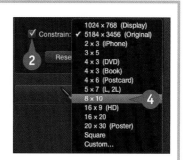

Rotate a Photo

You can rotate a photo using the iPhoto application, which comes with all new Macs as part of iLife, and is also available separately via the App Store. Depending on how you held your camera when you took a shot, the resulting photo might show the subject sideways or upside down. This may be the effect you want, but more likely this is a problem. To fix this problem, you can use iPhoto to rotate the photo so that the subject appears right-side up. You can rotate a photo either clockwise or counterclockwise.

Rotate a Photo

1 Click the photo you want to rotate.

Note: A quick way to rotate a photo is to right-click the photo and then click **Rotate** (🔄).

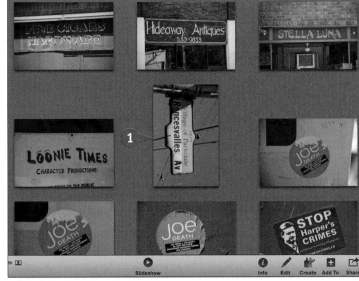

2 Click **Edit**.

iPhoto displays its editing tools.

3 Click Rotate (⟲).

A iPhoto rotates the photo 90 degrees counterclockwise.

4 Repeat step **3** until the subject of the photo is right-side up.

5 Click **Edit**.

iPhoto exits edit mode.

Can I rotate a photo clockwise instead?

Yes, you can rotate a photo clockwise by following these steps:

1 With the editing tools displayed, press and hold the Option key.

The Rotate icon changes from ⟲ to ⟳.

2 Press and hold Option and then click **Rotate** to rotate the photo clockwise by 90 degrees.

Note: You can also right-click the photo and then click **Rotate Clockwise**.

Straighten a Photo

You can straighten a crooked photo using the iPhoto application, which comes with all new Macs as part of iLife, and is also available separately via the App Store. If you do not use a tripod when taking pictures, getting your camera perfectly level when you take a shot is very difficult and requires a lot of practice and a steady hand. Despite your best efforts, you might end up with a photo that is not quite level. To fix this problem, you can use iPhoto to nudge the photo clockwise or counterclockwise so that the subject appears straight.

Straighten a Photo

① Click the photo you want to straighten.

② Click **Edit**.

iPhoto displays its editing tools.

③ Click **Straighten**.

iPhoto displays a grid over the photo.

④ Click and drag the **Angle** slider.

Drag the slider to the left to angle the photo counterclockwise.

Drag the slider to the right to angle the photo clockwise.

⑤ Click **Done**.

⑥ Click **Edit**.

iPhoto exits edit mode.

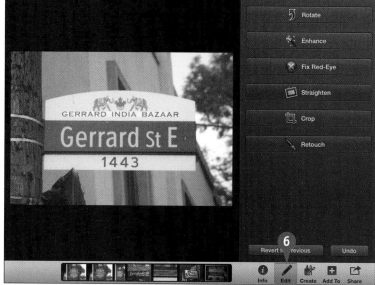

TIP

How do I know when my photo is level?

Use the gridlines that iPhoto places over the photo. Locate a horizontal line in your photo, and then rotate the photo so that this line is parallel to the nearest horizontal line in the grid. You can also match a vertical line in the photo with a vertical line in the grid.

Remove Red Eye from a Photo

You can remove red eye from a photo using the iPhoto application, which comes with all new Macs as part of iLife, and is also available separately via the App Store. When you use a flash to take a picture of one or more people, in some cases the flash may reflect off the subjects' retinas. The result is the common phenomenon of *red eye*, where each person's pupils appear red instead of black. If you have a photo where one or more people have red eyes due to the camera flash, you can use iPhoto to remove the red eye and give your subjects a more natural look.

Remove Red Eye from a Photo

1 Click the photo that contains the red eye.

2 Click **Edit**.

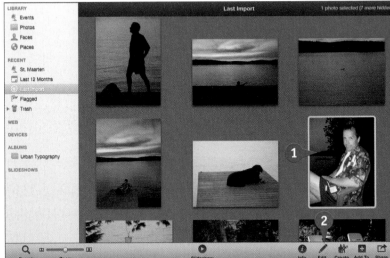

iPhoto displays its editing tools.

Ⓐ If needed, you can click and drag this slider to the right to zoom in on the picture.

Ⓑ You can click and drag this rectangle to bring the red eye into view.

3 Click **Fix Red-Eye**.

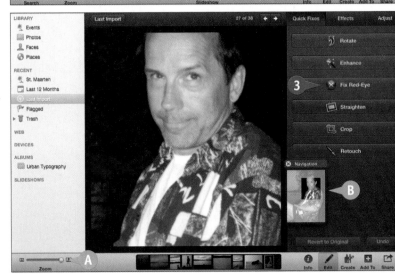

iPhoto displays its Red-Eye controls.

C You may be able to fix the red eye automatically by clicking the **Auto-fix red-eye** check box (☐ changes to ☑). If that does not work, continue with the rest of these steps.

4 Move the red-eye pointer over a red eye in the photo.

5 Click the red eye.

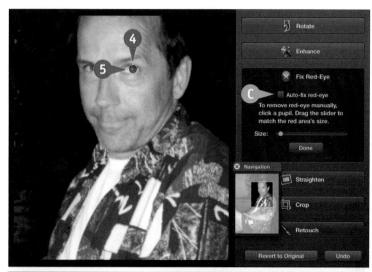

D iPhoto removes the red eye.

6 Repeat steps **4** and **5** to fix any other instances of red eye in the photo.

7 Click **Done**.

8 Click **Edit**.

iPhoto exits edit mode.

Why does iPhoto remove only part of the red eye in my photo?
The Red-Eye tool may not be set to a large enough size. The tool should be approximately the same size as the subject's eye:

1 Follow steps **1** to **3** to display the Red-Eye controls.

2 Click and drag the **Size** slider until the Red-Eye tool is the size of the red-eye area.

3 Use your mouse to move the circle over the red eye and then click.

Add Names to Faces in Your Photos

You can make your photos easier to manage and navigate by adding names to the faces that appear in each photo. This is sometimes called *tagging*, and it enables you to navigate your photos by name.

Specifically, iPhoto includes a special Faces section in its library, which organizes your faces according to the names you assign when you tag your photos. This makes it easy to view all your photos in which a certain person appears.

Add Names to Faces in Your Photos

1 Click the photo that you want to tag.

2 Click **Info**.

3 Click **X unnamed** (where *X* is the number of faces iPhoto identifies in the photo).

iPhoto displays its naming tools.

4 Click **unnamed**.

5 Type the person's name.

6 Press **Return**.

7 Repeat steps **3** to **5** to name each person in the photo.

Ⓐ If iPhoto did not mark a face in the photo, click **Add a face**, size and position the box over the face, and then type the name in the **click to name** box.

8 Click **Info**.

iPhoto exits naming mode.

How do I view all the photos that contain a particular person?

You can open a photo, click **Info**, and then click the **Show All** arrow (▣) beside the person's name. You can also follow these steps:

1 Click **Faces** in the iPhoto sidebar. iPhoto displays the names and sample photos of each person you have named.

2 Double-click the person you want to view. iPhoto displays all the photos that contain the person.

Map Your Photos

You can view your photos by location if you edit each photo to include the location where you took the image. Most modern cameras, particularly smartphone cameras such as those found on the iPhone and iPad, include location information for each photo. If your camera does not add location data automatically, you can tell iPhoto the locations where your photos were taken, and then display a map that shows those locations. This enables you to view all your photos taken in a particular place.

Map Your Photos

① Click the event that you want to map.

If you want to map a single photo, open the event and then open the photo.

② Click **Info**.

③ Click **Assign a Place**.

④ Type the location.

iPhoto displays a list of locations that match what you typed.

⑤ When you see the place you want to use, click it.

iPhoto displays the location on a Google map.

6 Click and drag the pin to the correct location, if necessary.

7 Click **Info**.

iPhoto closes the info window.

Is there a way to have the location data added automatically?

Yes. To activate this feature, click **iPhoto** in the menu bar, click **Preferences**, and then click the **Advanced** tab. Click the **Look up Places** ⁝ and then click **Automatically**. Note that you may still have to add or edit location names for your photos.

How do I view all the photos that were taken in a particular place?

Click **Places** in the iPhoto sidebar to see a map of the world with pins for each of your photo locations. Position the mouse (➤) over the location's pin, and then click the **Show All** arrow (◉). iPhoto displays all the photos that were taken in that location.

E-mail a Photo

If you have a photo that you want to share with someone, and you know that person's e-mail address, you can send the photo in an e-mail message. Using iPhoto, you can specify which photo you want to send, and iPhoto creates a new message. Even if a photo is very large, you can still send it via e-mail because you can use iPhoto to shrink the copy of the photo that appears in the message.

E-mail a Photo

1 Click the photo you want to send.

2 Click **Share**.

3 Click **Email**.

You can also click **Share** ( ) and then click **Email**.

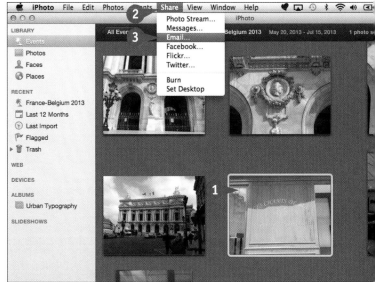

A iPhoto creates a new message and adds the photo to the message body.

4 Type the address of the message recipient.

5 Type the message subject.

6 Click here and then type your message text.

B You can use these controls to format the text.

C You can click these thumbnails to apply a special effect to the message.

7 Click **Send**.

iPhoto sends the message with the photo as an attachment.

TIP

How do I change the size of the photo?

You need to be careful when sending photos because a single image can be several megabytes in size. If your recipient's e-mail system places restrictions on the size of messages it can receive, your message might not go through.

To change the size of the photo, click the **Photo Size** ⁝ and then click the size you want to use for the sent photo, such as Small or Medium. Note that this does not affect the size of the original photo, just the copy that is sent with the message.

Take Your Picture

You can use your Mac to take a picture of yourself. If your Mac comes with a built-in iSight or FaceTime HD camera, or if you have an external camera attached to your Mac, you can use the camera to take a picture of yourself using the Photo Booth application. After you take your picture, you can e-mail that picture, add it to iPhoto, or set it as your user account or Messages buddy picture.

Take Your Picture

Take Your Picture with Photo Booth

1 In the Dock, click **Photo Booth** (🖼).

The Photo Booth window appears.

Ⓐ The live feed from the camera appears here.

2 Click **Take a still picture** (▢).

Ⓑ Click **Take four quick pictures** (▦) if you want Photo Booth to snap four successive photos, each about 1 second apart.

Ⓒ Click **Take a movie clip** (▣) if you want Photo Booth to capture the live camera feed as a movie.

③ Click **Take Photo** (◉).

Note: You can also press ⌘+T or click **File** and then click **Take Photo**.

Photo Booth counts down 3 seconds and then takes the photo.

Note: When the Mac is taking your picture, be sure to look into the camera, not into the screen.

Work with Your Photo Booth Picture

Ⓓ Photo Booth displays the picture.

① Click the picture.

② Click **Share** (☑).

Ⓔ Click **Add to iPhoto** to add the photo to iPhoto.

Ⓕ Click **Change profile picture** to set the photo as your user account picture.

TIP

Can I make my photos more interesting?
Definitely. Photo Booth comes with around two dozen special effects. Follow these steps:

① Click **Effects**.

② Click an icon to select a different page of effects.

Ⓐ You can also use the arrow buttons to change pages.

③ Click the effect you want to use.

CHAPTER 11

Playing and Creating Videos

Your Mac comes with the tools you need to play movies and digital video as well as to create your own digital videos.

Play a DVD Using DVD Player

If your Mac has a DVD drive, you can insert a movie DVD into the drive and then use the DVD Player application to play the movie on your Mac. You can either watch the movie in full-screen mode, where the movie takes up the entire Mac screen, or play the DVD in a window while you work on other things. DVD Player has features that enable you to control the movie playback and volume.

Play a DVD Using DVD Player

Play a DVD Full Screen

1 Insert the DVD into your Mac's DVD drive.

DVD Player runs automatically and starts playing the DVD full screen.

2 If you get to the DVD menu, click **Play** to start the movie.

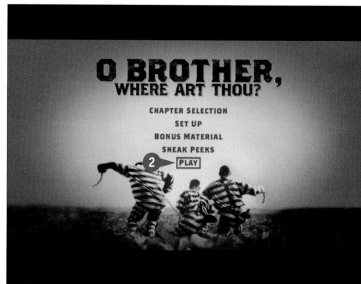

3 Move the mouse (🡤) to the bottom of the screen.

The playback controls appear.

Ⓐ Click to pause the movie.

Ⓑ Click to fast-forward the movie.

Ⓒ Click to rewind the movie.

Ⓓ Drag the slider to adjust the volume.

Ⓔ Click to display the DVD menu.

Ⓕ Click to exit full-screen mode.

Play a DVD in a Window

① Insert the DVD into your Mac's DVD drive.

DVD Player runs automatically and starts playing the DVD full screen.

② Press ⌘+F.

Note: You can also press Esc or move the ▶ to the bottom of the screen and then click **Exit full screen**.

DVD Player displays the movie in a window.

Ⓖ DVD Player displays the Controller.

③ When you get to the DVD menu, click **Play** to start the movie.

Ⓗ Click to pause the movie.

Ⓘ Click and hold to fast-forward the movie.

Ⓙ Click and hold to rewind the movie.

Ⓚ Drag the slider to adjust the volume.

Ⓛ Click to display the DVD menu.

Ⓜ Click to stop the movie.

Ⓝ Click to eject the DVD.

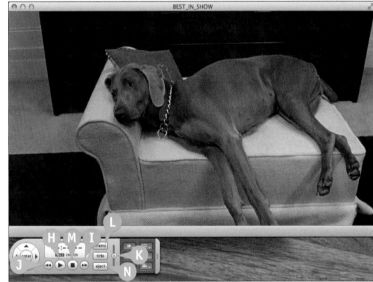

TIP

How can I always start my DVDs in a window?

① Press ⌘+F to switch to the window view.

② Click **DVD Player** in the menu bar.

③ Click **Preferences** to open the DVD Player preferences.

④ Click the **Player** tab.

⑤ Click **Enter Full Screen mode** (☑ changes to ☐).

⑥ To manually control when the playback starts, click **Start playing disc** (☑ changes to ☐).

⑦ Click **OK** to put the new settings into effect.

Play Digital Video with QuickTime Player

Your Mac comes with an application called QuickTime Player that can play digital video files in various formats. You will mostly use QuickTime Player to play digital video files stored on your Mac, but you can also use the application to play digital video from the web.

QuickTime Player enables you to open video files, navigate the digital video playback, and control the digital video volume. Although you learn only how to play digital video files in this section, the version of QuickTime that comes with OS X 10.9 (Mavericks) comes with many extra features, including the ability to record movies and audio and to cut and paste scenes.

Play Digital Video with QuickTime Player

1 Click **Finder** (☺).

2 Click **Applications**.

3 Double-click **QuickTime Player** (◎).

Note: If you see the **QuickTime Player** icon in the Dock, you can also click that icon to launch the program.

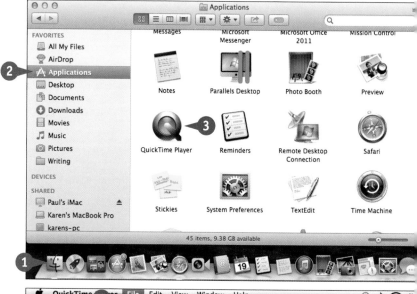

The QuickTime Player application appears.

4 Click **File**.

5 Click **Open File**.

Note: You can also press ⌘+O.

The Open dialog appears.

6 Locate and click the video file you want to play.

7 Click **Open**.

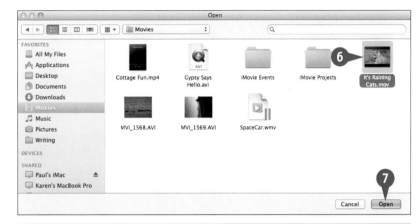

QuickTime opens a new player window.

8 Click **Play** (▶).

Ⓐ Click here to fast-forward the video.

Ⓑ Click here to rewind the video.

Ⓒ Click and drag this slider to adjust the volume.

If you want to view the video in full-screen mode, press ⌘+Ⓕ.

Can I use QuickTime Player to play a video from the web?
Yes. As long as you know the Internet address of the video, QuickTime Player can play most video formats available on the web. In QuickTime Player, click **File** and then click **Open Location** (or press ⌘+Ⓤ). In the Open URL dialog, type or paste the video address in the **Movie Location** text box, and then click **Open**.

Create a New Movie Project

The iLife suite installed on your Mac includes iMovie, which enables you to import video from a digital camcorder or video file and use that footage to create your own movies. You do this by first creating a project that holds your video clips, transitions, titles, and other elements of your movie.

When you first start iMovie, the program creates a new project for you automatically. Follow the steps in this section to create subsequent projects. Note, too, that iMovie is also available via the App Store.

Create a New Movie Project

① Click the **iMovie** icon (✶) in the Dock.

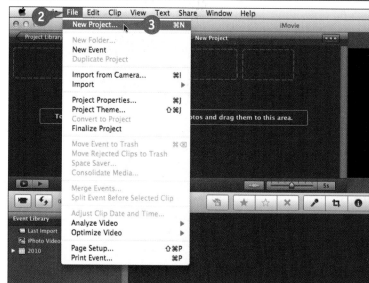

The iMovie window appears.

② Click **File**.

③ Click **New Project**.

Note: You can also press ⌘+Ⓝ.

The New Project dialog appears.

4 In the Name text box, type a name for your project.

5 Click the **Aspect Ratio** ⁝ and then click the ratio you prefer: Widescreen (16:9) or Standard (4:3).

6 To apply a theme to your project, click the one you want in the Project Themes list.

7 To automatically insert transitions between all your clips, click **Automatically add** (☐ changes to ☑) and then click ⁝ to choose the type of transition.

If you chose a theme in step **6**, the check box changes to **Automatically add transition and titles** by default.

8 Click **Create**.

iMovie creates your new project.

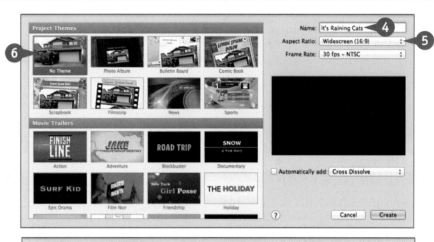

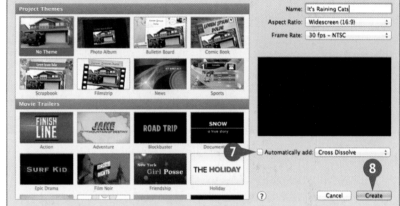

What are the iMovie themes?

iMovie offers seven themes that you can apply to a project. Each theme comes with its own set of titles and transitions that are added automatically. Among the themes are Photo Album, Bulletin Board, Comic Book, and Scrapbook. If one of them is suitable for your project, applying it can save on your production time.

How do I switch from one project to another?

You use the Project Library, which is a list of your movie projects. To display it, click **Window** and then click **Show Project Library**. You can also click the **Project Library** button in the top-left corner of the iMovie window. In the Project Library, double-click the project you want to work with.

Import a Video File

With the iMovie application, you can import digital video from a camera for use in your movie project. If you have video content on a USB digital camcorder or smartphone (such as an iPhone 3GS or later), you can connect the device to your Mac and then import some or all of the video to your iMovie project.

If your Mac or monitor has a built-in iSight or FaceTime HD camera, you can also use iMovie to import live images from that camera to use as digital video footage in your movie project.

Import a Video File

Import all Clips

1 Connect the video device to your Mac.

iMovie displays its Import From dialog.

2 Click **Import All**.

iMovie prompts you to create a new event.

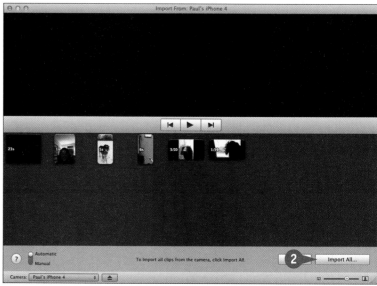

3 Click **Create new Event** (○ changes to ◉).

4 Use the Create new Event text box to type a name for the import event.

Ⓐ If you want to add the video to an existing event, click **Add to existing Event** (○ changes to ◉) and then choose the event from the pop-up menu.

5 Click **Import**.

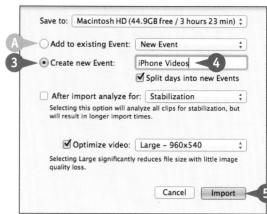

Import Selected Clips

1 Connect the video device to your Mac and place it in playback mode, if necessary.

iMovie displays its Import From dialog.

2 Click **Manual**.

3 Deselect the check box under each clip you do not want to import (☑ changes to ☐).

4 Click **Import Checked**.

iMovie prompts you to create a new event.

5 Click **Create new Event** (○ changes to ◉).

6 Use the Create new Event text box to type a name for the import event.

7 Click **Import**.

iMovie begins importing the clips.

8 Click **OK**.

9 Click **Done**.

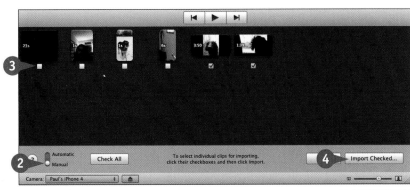

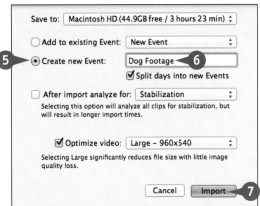

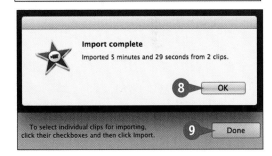

TIP

How do I import digital video from my iSight or FaceTime HD camera?

Follow these steps:

1 In iMovie, click **File** and then click **Import from Camera**.

2 Click **Capture**.

3 Follow steps **5** and **6** in the section "Import Selected Clips."

4 Click **Capture**.

5 When you are done, click **Stop**.

6 Click **Done**.

Add Video Clips to Your Project

To create and work with a movie project in iMovie, you must first add some video clips to that project. A *video clip* is a segment of digital video. You begin building your movie by adding one o more video clips to your project.

When you import digital video as described in the previous section, iMovie automatically breaks up the video into separate clips, with each clip being the footage shot during a single recording session. You can then decide which of those clips you want to add to your project, or you can add only part of a clip.

Add Video Clips to Your Project

Add an Entire Clip

1 Click the Event Library item that contains the video clip you want to add.

2 Press and hold **Option** and click the clip.

Ⓐ iMovie selects the entire clip.

3 Click and drag the selected clip and drop it in your project at the spot where you want the clip to appear.

Ⓑ iMovie adds the entire video clip to the project.

Ⓒ iMovie adds an orange bar to the bottom of the original clip to indicate that it has been added to the project.

Add a Partial Clip

1 Click the Event Library item that contains the video clip you want to add.

2 Click the clip at the point where you want the selection to begin.

3 Click and drag the right edge of the selection box to the point where you want the selection to end.

4 Click and drag the selected clip and drop it in your project at the spot where you want the clip to appear.

Ⓓ iMovie adds the selected portion of the video clip to the project.

Ⓔ iMovie adds an orange bar to the bottom of the original clip to indicate that it has been added to a project.

TIPS

Is it possible to play a clip before I add it?
Yes. The easiest way to do this is to click the clip at the point where you want the playback to start and then press Spacebar. iMovie plays the clip in the Viewer in the top-right corner of the window. Press Spacebar again to stop the playback.

I added a clip in the wrong place. Can I move it?
Yes. In your project, click the added clip to select it. Use your mouse (▶) to click and drag the clip and then drop the clip in the correct location within the project. If you want to delete the clip from the project, click it, click **Edit**, and then click **Delete Entire Clip** (or press Option + Delete).

Trim a Clip

If you have a video clip that is too long or contains footage you do not need, you can shorten the clip or remove the extra footage. Removing parts of a video clip is called *trimming* the clip.

Trimming a clip is particularly useful if you recorded extra, unneeded footage before and after the action you were trying to capture. By trimming this unneeded footage, your movie will include only the material you really require.

Trim a Clip

① In your project, click the clip you want to trim.

Ⓐ iMovie selects the entire clip.

② Use your mouse (▶) to click and drag the left edge of the selection box to the starting position of the part of the clip you want to keep.

③ Use your mouse (▶) to click and drag the right edge of the selection box to the ending position of the part of the clip you want to keep.

④ Click **Clip**.

⑤ Click **Trim to Selection**.

Note: You can also press ⌘+B.

Ⓑ iMovie trims the clip.

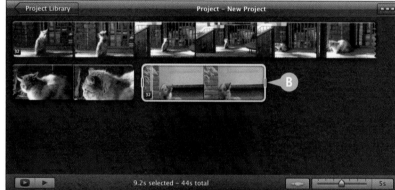

TIP

How can I trim one frame at a time from either the beginning or the end of the clip?

① In your project, click the clip you want to trim.

② Click **Clip**.

③ Click **Trim Clip End**.

④ Select the trim direction by clicking **Move Left** or **Move Right**.

⑤ Repeat step 4 until you reach the number of frames that you want to trim.

Add a Transition Between Clips

You can use the iMovie application to enhance the visual appeal of your digital movie by inserting transitions between some or all of the project's video clips. By default, iMovie jumps immediately from the end of one clip to the beginning of the next clip, a transition called a *jump cut*. You can add more visual interest to your movie by adding a transition between the two clips.

iMovie offers 24 different transitions, including various fades, wipes, and dissolves. More transitions are available if you applied a theme to your iMovie project.

Add a Transition Between Clips

① Click the **Transitions Browser** button (▣), or press ⌘+④.

Ⓐ iMovie displays the available transitions.

Note: To see a preview of a transition, position your mouse (►) over the transition thumbnail.

② Use your mouse (►) to click and drag a transition and drop it between the two clips.

220

B iMovie adds an icon for the transition between the two clips.

3 Position your mouse (🡔) over the beginning of the transition and move the 🡔 to the right.

C iMovie displays a preview of the transition.

How can I change the duration of the transition?

1 Double-click the transition icon in your project.

The Inspector appears.

2 Use the Duration text box to set the number of seconds you want the transition to take.

3 If you want to change only the current transition, click **Applies to all transitions** (☑ changes to ☐).

4 Click **Done**.

Add a Photo

You can use the iMovie application to enhance your movie projects with still photos. Although most movie projects consist of several video clips, you can also add a photo to your project. By default, iMovie displays the photo for 4 seconds.

You can also specify how the photo fits in the movie frame: You can adjust the size of the photo to fit the frame, you can crop the photo, or you can apply a Ken Burns effect to animate the static photo, which automatically pans and zooms the photo.

Add a Photo

① Click the **Photos Browser** button (📷), or press ⌘+②.

Ⓐ iMovie displays the available photos.

② Click the event or album that contains the photo you want to add.

③ Click and drag the photo and drop it inside your project.

Ⓑ iMovie adds the photo to the movie.

④ Click the photo.

⑤ Click the **Crop** button (🔳).

iMovie displays the cropping
options for the photo.

6 Click **Ken Burns**.

C You can also click **Fit** to have
iMovie adjust the size of the photo
to fit the movie frame.

D You can also click **Crop** and then
click and drag the cropping
rectangle to specify how much of
the photo you want to appear in
the movie frame.

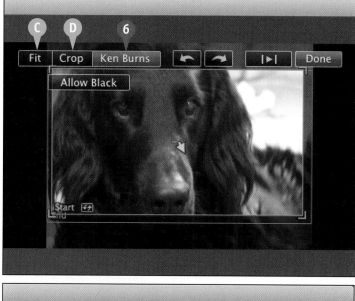

7 Click and drag the green rectangle
to set the start point of the Ken
Burns animation.

8 Click and drag the red rectangle to
set the end point of the Ken Burns
animation.

Note: Click and drag the corners and
edges of the rectangle to change the
size; click and drag the interior of the
rectangles to change the position.

E The arrow shows the direction of
motion.

9 Click **Done**.

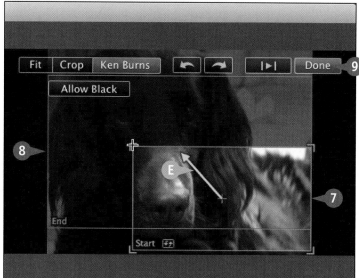

TIP

How can I change the length of time that the photo appears in the movie?

1 Double-click the photo in your
project.

2 Click **Clip**.

3 Use the Duration text box to
set the number of seconds you
want the photo to appear.

4 To change the duration for all the
photos in your project, click
Applies to all stills (☐ changes
to ☑).

5 Click **Done**.

Add a Music Track

Using the iMovie application, you can enhance the audio component of your movie by adding one or more songs that play in the background. With iMovie you can also add sound effects and other audio files that you feel would enhance your project's audio track.

To get the best audio experience, you can adjust various sound properties. For example, you can adjust the volume of the music clip or the volume of the video clip. You can also use iMovie to adjust the time it takes for the song clip to fade in and fade out.

Add a Music Track

1. Click the **Music and Sound Effect Browser** button (🎵), or press ⌘ + 1 .

Ⓐ iMovie displays the available audio files.

2. Click the folder, category, or playlist that contains the track you want to add.

3. Use your mouse (➤) to click and drag the song and drop it on a video clip.

Ⓑ iMovie adds the song to the movie.

Note: iMovie treats the song like a clip, which means you can trim the song as needed, as described earlier in the section "Trim a Clip."

4. Double-click the music clip.

iMovie displays the Inspector.

5 Click the **Audio** tab.

6 Use the **Volume** slider to adjust the volume of the music clip.

7 If you want to reduce the video clip volume, click **Ducking** (☐ changes to ☑) and then click and drag the slider.

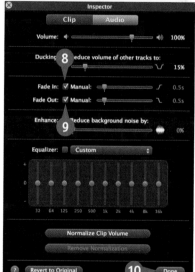

8 To adjust the fade-in time, click **Fade In: Manual** (☐ changes to ☑) and then click and drag the slider.

9 To adjust the fade-out time, click **Fade Out: Manual** (☐ changes to ☑) and then click and drag the slider.

10 Click **Done**.

TIP

When I add a video clip before the music clip, the music does not play with the new video clip. How can I work around this?

You need to add your song as a background track instead of a clip. Click ♫ (Ⓐ). Click and drag a song onto the project background (Ⓑ), not on a clip or between two clips. The background turns green when the song is positioned correctly (Ⓒ).

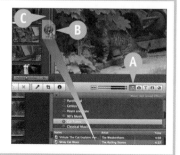

Record a Voiceover

You can use the iMovie application to augment the audio portion of your movie with a voiceover. A *voiceover* is a voice recording that you make using audio equipment attached to your Mac.

A voiceover is useful for explaining a video clip, introducing the movie, or giving the viewer background information about the movie. To record a voiceover, your Mac must have either a built-in microphone, such as the one that comes with the iSight or FaceTime HD camera, or an external microphone connected via an audio jack, USB port, or Bluetooth.

Record a Voiceover

① If your Mac does not have a built-in microphone, attach a microphone.

Note: You may need to configure the microphone as the sound input device. Click **System Preferences** (), click **Sound**, click **Input**, and then click your microphone.

② Click the **Voiceover** button ().

The Voiceover dialog appears.

③ Click the spot in the movie at which you want the voiceover to begin.

226

iMovie counts down and then begins the recording.

④ Speak your voiceover text into the microphone.

Ⓐ The progress of the recording appears here.

⑤ When you finish, click **Recording**.

Ⓑ iMovie adds the voiceover to the clip.

⑥ Click **Close** (🗙).

You can double-click the voiceover to adjust the audio, as described in the previous section.

Is there a way to tell if my voice is too loud or too soft?

Yes. You can use the controls in the Voiceover dialog to check your voice level by talking into the microphone and then watching the Left and Right volume meters. No green bars or just a few green bars indicate the voice level is too low (Ⓐ). Yellow or red bars indicate the voice level is too high (Ⓑ). Use the Input Volume slider to adjust the voice level up or down, as needed.

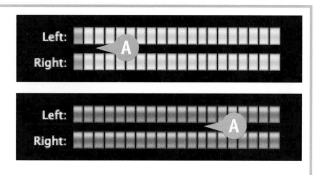

Add Titles and Credits

Y ou can use the iMovie application to enhance your movie project with titles and scrolling credits. You can get your movie off to a proper start by adding a title and a subtitle at or near the beginning of the movie. iMovie offers a number of title styles from which you can choose, and you can also change the title font.

You can also enhance your movie with *scrolling credits*. This is a special type of title that you place at the end of the movie and that scrolls the names of the people responsible for the project.

Add Titles and Credits

1 Click the **Titles browser** button (**T**).

A iMovie displays the available title types.

2 Use your mouse (**k**) to click and drag a title and drop it where you want the titles to appear.

Note: To see just the titles, drop the title thumbnail at the beginning of the movie or between two clips. To superimpose the titles on a video clip, drop the title thumbnail on the clip.

B If you want to add credits, click and drag the **Scrolling Credits** thumbnail and drop it at the end of the movie.

C iMovie adds a clip for the title.

3 Replace this text with the movie title.

4 Replace this text with the movie subtitle.

5 Click **Done**.

Note: iMovie treats the title like a clip, which means you can lengthen or shorten the title duration by clicking and dragging the beginning or end, as described earlier in the section "Trim a Clip."

How do I change the font of the titles?

The Text menu offers several font-related commands, including Bold, Italic, Bigger, and Smaller. You can also click the **Show Fonts** command to display the Choose Font dialog. If you do not see the Choose Font dialog shown here, you can switch to iMovie's predefined fonts by clicking **iMovie Font Panel**. You can then click a typeface, font color, and type size; click **Done** to close the dialog.

Play the Movie

The iMovie application offers the Viewer pane, which you can use to play your movie. While you are building your iMovie project, it is a good idea to occasionally play some or all of the movie to check your progress. For example, you can play the entire movie to make sure the video and audio are working properly and are synchronized correctly. You can also play parts of the movie to ensure that your transitions appear when you want them to.

Play the Movie

Play from the Beginning

1 Click **View**.

2 Click **Play from Beginning**.

Note: You can also press or click the **Play Project from beginning** button ().

Play from a Specific Location

1 Position the mouse () over the spot where you want to start playing the movie.

2 Press Spacebar.

Play a Selection

1 Select the video clips you want to play.

Note: See the first Tip to learn how to select multiple video clips.

2 Click **View**.

3 Click **Play Selection**.

Note: You can also press [/].

TIPS

How do I select multiple video clips?

To select multiple video clips, press and hold ⌘ and then click anywhere inside each clip you want to select. If you select a clip by accident, ⌘+click it again to deselect it. If you want to skip just a few clips, first press ⌘+A to select all the clips, then press and hold ⌘ and click the clips you do not want in the selection.

Can I enlarge the size of the playback pane?

Yes, you can play your movie in full-screen mode. To do this, click **View** and then click **Play full-screen**. You can also press ⌘+G or click the **Play Project full screen** button (▣).

231

Publish Your Movie to YouTube

When your movie project is complete, you can send it to YouTube for viewing on the web. To publish your movie to YouTube, you must have a YouTube account, available from www.youtube.com. You must also know your YouTube username, which you can see by clicking your account icon on YouTube and then clicking Settings. Your movie must be no more than 15 minutes long. Before you can publish your movie, you must select a YouTube category, such as Entertainment or Pets and Animals, provide a title and description, and enter at least one tag, which is a word or short phrase that describes some aspect of the movie's content.

Publish Your Movie to YouTube

1 Click **Share**.

2 Click **YouTube**.

3 Click **Add**.

iMovie prompts you for your YouTube username.

④ Type your username.

⑤ Click **Done** (not shown).

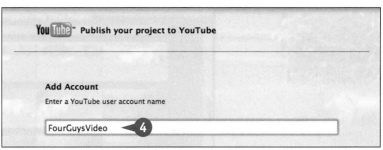

⑥ Type your YouTube password.

⑦ Select a category.

⑧ Type a title.

⑨ Type a description.

⑩ Type one or more tags for the video.

⑪ If you do not want to allow anyone to view the movie, click **Make this movie personal** (☑ changes to ☐).

⑫ Click **Next**.

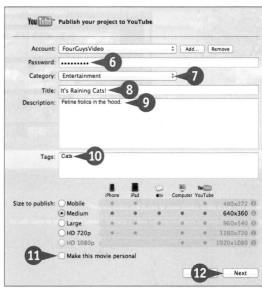

iMovie displays the YouTube terms of service.

⑬ Click **Publish**.

iMovie prepares the movie and then publishes it to YouTube.

⑭ Click **OK** (not shown).

TIPS

How do I publish my movie to Facebook?
Click **Share** and then click **Facebook**. Click **Add**, type your Facebook e-mail address, and then click **Done**. Type your Facebook password. Use the **Viewable by** pop-up menu to choose who can see the video. Type a title and description, select a size, click **Next**, and then click **Publish**.

How do I view my movie outside of iMovie?
Beyond viewing it on YouTube or Facebook, you need to export the movie to a digital video file. Click **Share** and then click **Export Movie** (or press ⌘+E). Type a title for the movie, and then click a **Size to Export** option, such as Large or HD 720p (○ changes to ⊙). Click **Export**.

CHAPTER 12

Customizing OS X

OS X comes with a number of features that enable you to customize your Mac. For example, you might not like the default desktop background or the layout of the Dock. Not only can you change the appearance of OS X to suit your taste, but you can also change the way OS X works to make it easier and more efficient for you to use.

Display System Preferences

You can find many of the OS X customization features in System Preferences, a collection of settings and options that control the overall look and operation of OS X. You can use System Preferences to change the desktop background, specify a screen saver, set your Mac's sleep options, add user accounts, and customize the Dock, to name some of the tasks that you learn about in this chapter. To use these settings, you must know how to display the System Preferences window.

Display System Preferences

Open System Preferences

1 In the Dock, click **System Preferences** ( ).

The System Preferences window appears.

lose System Preferences

1 Click **System Preferences**.

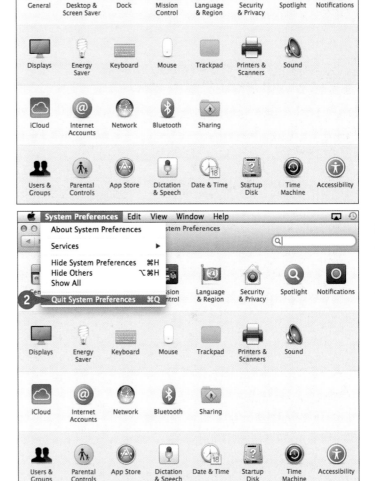

2 Click **Quit System Preferences**.

Are there other methods I can use to open System Preferences?

If you have hidden the Dock or removed the System Preferences icon from the Dock, you can click and then click **System Preferences**.

Sometimes when I open System Preferences, I do not see all the icons. How can I restore the original icons?

When you click an icon in System Preferences, the window changes to show just the options and settings associated with that icon. To return to the main System Preferences window, click **View** and then click **Show All Preferences** (or press ⌘+L). You can also click ◄ until the main window appears, or click **Show All**.

Change the Desktop Background

To give OS X a different look, you can change the default desktop background. OS X offers a wide variety of desktop background options. For example, OS X comes with several dozen images you can use, from abstract patterns to photos of plants and other natural images. You can also choose a solid color as the desktop background, or you can use one of your own photos. You can change the desktop background to show either a fixed image or a series of images that change periodically.

Change the Desktop Background

Set a Fixed Background Image

1 In the Dock, click **System Preferences** (⚙).

2 In the System Preferences window, click **Desktop & Screen Saver**.

Note: You can also right-click the desktop and then click **Change Desktop Background**.

The desktop and screen saver preferences appear.

3 Click **Desktop**.

4 Click the image category you want to use.

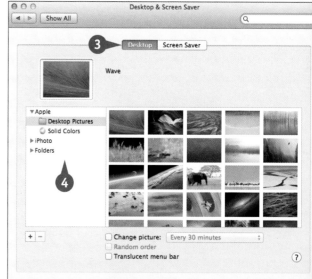

5 Click the image you want to use as the desktop background.

Your Mac changes the desktop background.

6 If you chose a photo in step **5**, click ⁞ and then click an option to determine how your Mac displays the photo.

Note: Another way to set a fixed background image is to select a photo in iPhoto, click **Share**, and then click **Set Desktop**.

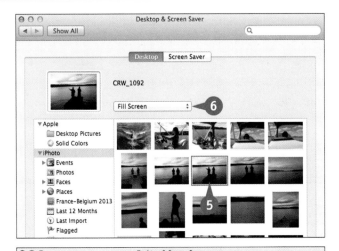

Set a Changing Background Image

1 Click **Change picture** (☐ changes to ☑).

2 Click ⁞ in the pop-up menu and then click how often you want the background image to change.

3 If you want your Mac to choose the periodic image randomly, click **Random order** (☐ changes to ☑).

Your Mac changes the desktop background periodically based on your chosen interval.

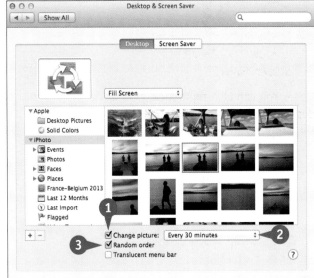

TIP

When I choose a photo, how do the various options differ for displaying the photo?

Your Mac gives you five options for displaying the photo:

- **Fill Screen.** Expands the photo in all four directions until it fills the entire desktop.
- **Fit to Screen.** Expands the photo in all four directions until the photo is either the same height as the desktop or the same width as the desktop.
- **Stretch to Fill Screen.** Expands the photo in all four directions until it fills the entire desktop.
- **Center.** Displays the photo at its actual size and places the photo in the center of the desktop.
- **Tile.** Repeats your photo multiple times to fill the entire desktop.

Activate the Screen Saver

You can set up OS X to display a *screen saver*, a moving pattern or series of pictures. The screen saver appears after your computer has been idle for a while. If you leave your monitor on for long stretches while your computer is idle, a faint version of the unmoving image can endure for a while on the screen, a phenomenon known as *persistence*. A screen saver prevents this by displaying a moving image. However, persistence is not a major problem for modern screens, so for the most part you use a screen saver for visual interest.

Activate the Screen Saver

1 In the Dock, click **System Preferences** (⚙).

2 In the System preferences window, click **Desktop & Screen Saver**.

The Desktop & Screen Saver dialog appears.

3 Click **Screen Saver**.

4 Click the screen saver you want to use.

Ⓐ A preview of the screen saver appears here.

⑤ Click the **Start after** ⬍ and
then click a time delay until
the screen saver begins.

ote: The interval you choose is
he number of minutes or hours
hat your Mac must be idle before
he screen saver starts.

Ⓑ If the screen saver is
customizable, click **Screen
Saver Options** to configure it.

Ⓒ If you chose a slide show
instead of a screen saver, click
the **Source** ⬍ to select an
image collection.

Ⓓ If you also want to see the
current time when the screen
saver is active, click **Show with
clock** (☐ changes to ☑).

TIP

What are hot corners and how do I configure them?
A *hot corner* is a corner of your Mac's screen that you have set up to perform an action when you move the
mouse (🖈) to that specific corner. To configure hot corners, follow steps **1** to **4** to select a screen saver, In
the lower-left of the dialog, click **Hot Corners**. In the Active Screen Corners dialog, click the upper-left spin
arrows (⬍) and select the action you want to perform when you move mouse (🖈) to the top-left corner of
the screen. Click the spin arrows (⬍) for the remaining corners and select the action you want to perform
when you move mouse (🖈) to the specific corner of the screen.

Set Your Mac's Sleep Options

You can make OS X more energy efficient by configuring parts of your Mac to go into sleep mode automatically when you are not using them. *Sleep mode* means that your display or your Mac is in a temporary low-power mode. This saves energy on all Macs, and saves battery power on a notebook Mac. For example, you can set up OS X to put the display to sleep automatically after a period of inactivity. Similarly, you can configure OS X to put your entire Mac to sleep after you have not used it for a specified amount of time.

Set Your Mac's Sleep Options

Open the Energy Saver Preferences

1 In the Dock, click **System Preferences** (⚙).

2 In the System Preferences window, click **Energy Saver**.

The Energy Saver preferences appear.

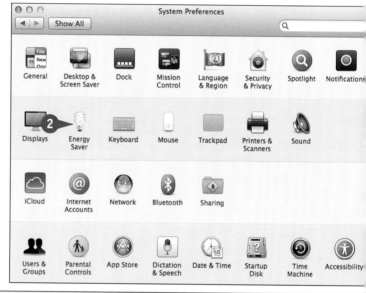

Set Sleep Options for a Desktop Mac

1 Click and drag ▽ to set the computer sleep timer.

This specifies the period of inactivity after which your computer goes to sleep.

2 Click and drag ▽ to set the display sleep timer.

This specifies the period of inactivity after which your display goes to sleep.

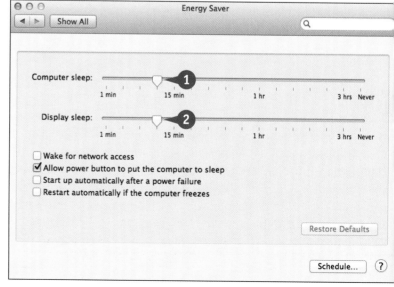

et Sleep Options for a otebook Mac

1 Click **Battery**.

2 Click and drag ▽ to set the computer sleep timer for when your Mac is on battery power.

3 Click and drag ▽ to set the display sleep timer for when your Mac is on battery power.

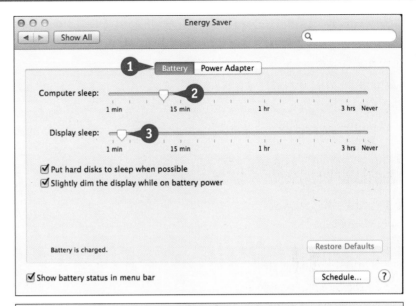

4 Click **Power Adapter**.

5 Click and drag ▽ to set the computer sleep timer for when your Mac is plugged in.

6 Click and drag ▽ to set the display sleep timer for when your Mac is plugged in.

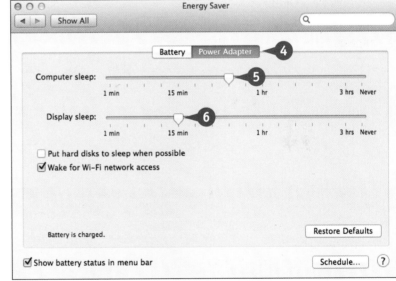

TIPS

How do I wake a sleeping display or computer?

If your Mac's display is in sleep mode, you can wake it by moving your mouse or sliding your finger on the trackpad. You can also wake up the display or your entire Mac by pressing any key.

I changed the display sleep timer, now I never see my screen saver. Why?

You set the display sleep timer to a time that is less than your screen saver timer. Suppose you configured OS X to switch on the screen saver after 15 minutes. If you set the display sleep timer to a shorter interval, such as 10 minutes, OS X always puts the display to sleep before the screen saver appears.

Change the Display Resolution and Brightness

You can change the resolution and the brightness of the OS X display. This enables you to adjust the display for best viewing or for maximum compatibility with whatever application you are using.

Increasing the display resolution is an easy way to create more space on the screen for applications and windows, because the objects on the screen appear smaller. Conversely, if you have trouble reading text on the screen, decreasing the display resolution can help, because the screen objects appear larger. If you find that your display is too dark or too bright, you can adjust the brightness for best viewing.

Change the Display Resolution and Brightness

1 In the Dock, click **System Preferences** (📷).

2 In the System Preferences window, click **Displays**.

The Displays preferences appear.

3 Click **Display**.

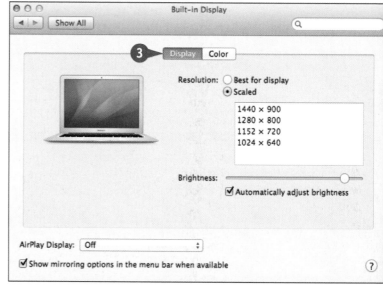

4 Select the resolution:

A To have OS X set the resolution based on your display, click **Best for display** (○ changes to ⊙).

B To set the resolution yourself, click **Scaled** (○ changes to ⊙) and then click the resolution you want to use.

OS X adjusts the screen to the new resolution.

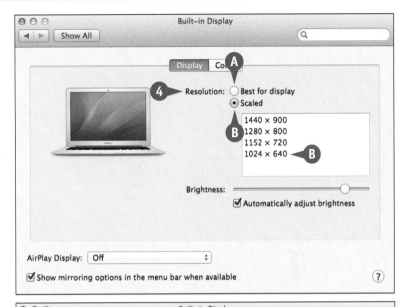

5 Click and drag the **Brightness** slider to set the display brightness.

OS X adjusts the screen to the new brightness.

C If you do not want OS X to adjust the brightness based on the ambient light, click **Automatically adjust brightness** (☑ changes to ☐).

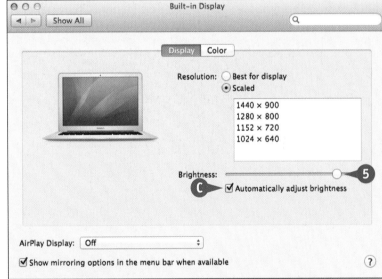

TIPS

What do the resolution numbers mean?

The resolution numbers are expressed in *pixels*, short for picture elements, which are the individual dots that make up what you see on your Mac's screen, arranged in rows and columns. So a resolution of 1440 × 900 means that the display is using 1,440-pixel rows and 900-pixel columns.

Why do some resolutions also include the word stretched?

Most older displays use an aspect ratio (width to the height) of 4:3. However, most new Mac displays use an aspect ratio of 16:10, which is called *widescreen*. Resolutions designed for 4:3 displays take up only part of a widescreen display. To make them take up the entire display, choose the *stretched* version of the resolution.

Create an App Folder in Launchpad

Y**ou can make Launchpad easier to use by combining multiple icons into a single storage area called** an *app folder*. Normally, Launchpad displays icons in up to five rows per screen, with at least seven icons in each row, so you can have at least 35 icons in each screen. Also, if you have configured your Mac with a relatively low display resolution, you might see only partial app names in Launchpad.

All this can make it difficult to locate your apps. However, app folders can help you organize similar apps and reduce the clutter on the Launchpad screens.

Create an App Folder in Launchpad

1 Click **Launchpad** ( ).

A Launchpad displays icons for each installed application.

2 Click the dot for the Launchpad screen with which you want to work.

3 Use the ▶ to click and drag an icon that you want to include in the folder, and drop it on another icon that you want to include in the same folder.

246

B Launchpad creates the app folder.

C Launchpad applies a name to the folder based on the type of applications in the folder.

D Launchpad adds the icons to the app folder.

4 To specify a different name, click the name and then type the one you prefer.

5 Click the Launchpad screen, outside of the app folder.

E Launchpad displays the app folder.

6 To add more icons to the new app folder, use the ⬆ to click and drag each icon and drop it on the folder.

Note: To launch a program from an app folder, click ⬤, click the app folder to open it, and then click the program's icon.

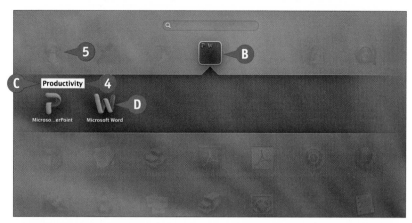

TIPS

How do I make changes to an app folder?
Click ⬤ to open Launchpad, then click the app folder. To rename the app folder, click the current name, type the new name, and then press `Return`. To rearrange the icons, use the ⬆ to drag and drop the apps within the folder. When you are done, click outside the app folder to close it.

How do I remove an icon from an app folder?
Click ⬤ to open Launchpad, then click the app folder. To remove an app from a folder, use the ⬆ to click and drag the app out of the folder. Launchpad closes the folder, and you can then drop the icon within the Launchpad screen.

Add a User Account

You can share your Mac with another person by creating a user account for that person. This enables the person to log in to OS X and use the system. The new user account is completely separate from your own account. This means that the other person can change settings, create documents, and perform other OS X tasks without interfering with your own settings or data. For maximum privacy for all users, you should set up each user account with a password.

Add a User Account

1 In the Dock, click **System Preferences** ( ).

2 In the System Preferences window, click **Users & Groups**.

Ⓐ In most OS X systems, to modify accounts you must click the **Lock** icon ( ) and then type your administrator password (changes to).

3 Click **Add** ( ).

The New Account dialog appears.

④ Click ⬦ and then click an account type.

⑤ Type the user's name.

⑥ Edit the short username that OS X creates.

⑦ Type a password for the user.

⑧ Retype the user's password.

⑨ Type a hint that OS X will display if the user forgets the password.

⑩ Click **Create User**.

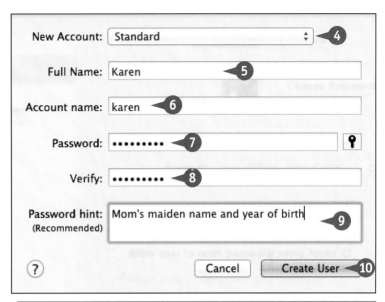

Ⓑ OS X adds the user account to the Users & Groups preferences window.

TIPS

Which account type should I use for the new account?

The Standard account type is a good choice because it can make changes only to its own account settings. Avoid the Administrator option because it is a powerful account type that enables the user to make major changes to the system. If the user is a child, consider the Managed with Parental Controls account type.

How do I change the user's picture?

In the Users & Groups preferences, click the user and then click the picture. OS X displays a list of the available images. If you see one you like, click it. If your Mac has a camera attached and the user is nearby, you can click **Camera** and then click the **Camera** icon to take the user's picture. Click **Done** to set the picture.

Customize the Dock

You can customize various aspects of the Dock by using System Preferences to modify a few Dock options. For example, you can make the Dock take up less room on the screen by adjusting the size of the Dock. You can also make the Dock a bit easier to use by turning on the Magnification feature, which enlarges Dock icons when you position the mouse pointer over them. You can also make the Dock easier to access and use by moving it to either side of the screen.

Customize the Dock

1 In the Dock, click **System Preferences** (⚙).

2 In the System Preferences window, click **Dock**.

Note: You can also open the Dock preferences by clicking , clicking **Dock**, and then clicking **Dock Preferences**.

The Dock preferences appear.

3 Click and drag the **Size** slider (▽) to make the Dock smaller or larger.

Ⓐ You can also click and drag the Dock divider: Drag up to increase the Dock size, and drag down to decrease the Dock size.

Ⓑ System Preferences adjusts the size of the Dock.

Note: If your Dock is already as wide as the screen, dragging the Size slider to the right (toward the Large value) has no effect.

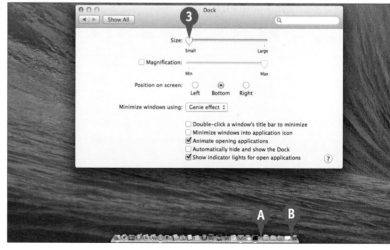

4 Click **Magnification** (☐ changes to ☑).

5 Click and drag the **Magnification** ▽ to set the magnification level.

C When you position the mouse (▶) over a Dock icon, your Mac magnifies the icon.

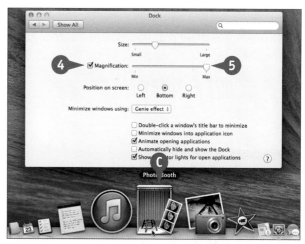

6 Use the **Position on screen** options to click where you want the Dock to appear, such as the **Left** side of the screen (○ changes to ◉).

D Your Mac moves the Dock to the new position.

7 In the **Minimize windows using** pop-up menu, click ⬍ and then click the effect you want your Mac to use when you minimize a window: **Genie effect** or **Scale effect**.

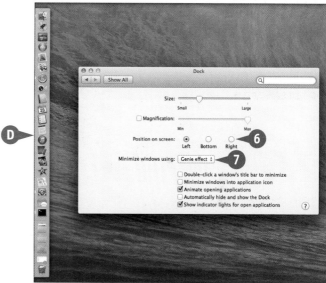

<hr>

TIP

Is there an easier method I can use to control some of these preferences?
Yes, you can control these preferences directly from the Dock. To set the Dock size, click and drag the Dock divider left or right. For the other preferences, right-click the Dock divider. Click **Turn Magnification On** to enable the magnification feature; click **Turn Magnification Off** to disable this feature. To change the Dock position, click **Position on Screen** and then click **Left**, **Bottom**, or **Right**. To set the minimize effect, click **Minimize Using** and then click either **Genie Effect** or **Scale Effect**. Finally, you can also click **Dock Preferences** to open the Dock pane in System Preferences.

Add an Icon to the Dock

The icons on the Dock are convenient because you can open them with just a single click. You can enhance the convenience of the Dock by adding an icon for an application you use frequently.

The icon remains in the Dock even when the application is closed, so you can always open the application with a single click. You can add an icon to the Dock even if the program is not currently running.

Add an Icon to the Dock

Add an Icon for a Nonrunning Application

1 Click **Finder** (🖼️).

2 Click **Applications**.

3 Click and drag the application icon, and then drop it inside the Dock.

🅐 Be sure to drop the icon anywhere to the left of the Dock divider.

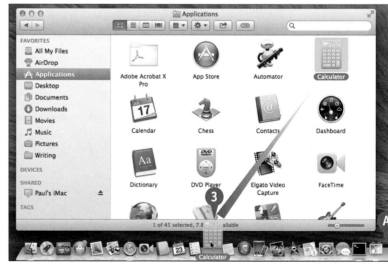

B OS X adds the application's icon to the Dock.

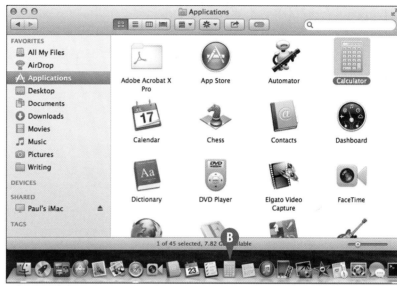

Add an Icon for a Running Application

1 Right-click the application icon in the Dock.

2 Click **Options**.

3 Click **Keep in Dock**.

The application's icon remains in the Dock even after you close the program.

TIPS

Can my Mac start the application automatically each time I log in?
Yes. Your Mac maintains a list of *login items*, which are applications that run automatically after you log in. You can configure your application as a login item, and your Mac opens it automatically each time you log in. Right-click the application's Dock icon, click **Options**, and then click **Open at Login**.

How do I remove an icon from the Dock?
Right-click the application's Dock icon, click **Options**, and then click **Remove from Dock**. If the application is currently running, OS X removes the icon from the Dock when you quit the program. Note that you can remove any application icon except Finder (🖼) and Launchpad (🚀).

Hide the Dock

When you are working in an application, you might find that you need to maximize the amount of vertical space the application window takes up on-screen. This might come up, for example, when you are reading or editing a long document or viewing a large photo. In such cases, you can size the window to maximum height, but OS X will not let you go past the Dock. You can work around this by hiding the Dock. When the Dock is hidden, it is still easily accessible whenever you need to use it.

Hide the Dock

Turn On Dock Hiding

1 Click .

2 Click **Dock**.

3 Click **Turn Hiding On**.

Ⓐ You can also right-click the Dock divider and then click **Turn Hiding On**.

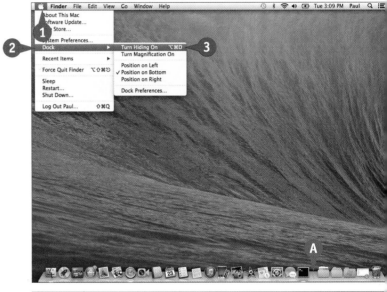

Ⓑ OS X removes the Dock from the desktop.

Display the Dock Temporarily

1 Move the mouse (➤) to the bottom of the screen.

C OS X temporarily displays the Dock.

Note: To hide the Dock again, move the mouse (➤) away from the bottom of the screen.

TIPS

Is there a faster way to hide the Dock?
Yes. You can quickly hide the Dock by pressing
Option + ⌘ + D . This keyboard shortcut is a toggle,
which means that you can also turn off Dock hiding
by pressing Option + ⌘ + D . When the Dock is
hidden, you can display it temporarily by pressing
Control + F3 (on some keyboards you must press
Fn + Control + F3).

How do I bring the Dock back into view?
When you no longer need the extra screen space for
your applications, you can turn off Dock hiding to
bring the Dock back into view. Click , click **Dock**,
and then click **Turn Hiding Off**. Alternatively,
display the Dock, right-click the Dock divider, and
then click **Turn Hiding Off**.

Add a Widget to the Dashboard

The Dashboard is an OS X application that you use to display widgets. You can customize the Dashboard to include any widgets that you find useful or informative. A widget is a mini-application, particularly one designed to perform a single task, such as displaying the weather, showing stock data, or providing sports scores. OS X comes with 16 widgets, which include a clock, a calculator, a tile game, and a unit converter. There are also many widgets available online.

Add a Widget to the Dashboard

1 Click **Finder** ( ).

2 Click **Applications**.

3 Double-click **Dashboard** ( ).

Your Mac displays the Dashboard and its current set of open widgets.

4 Click **Add** ( ).

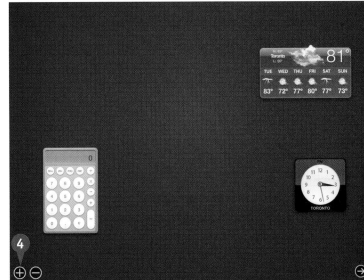

OS X displays its collection of widgets.

⑤ Click the widget you want to add.

Ⓐ Your Mac adds the widget to the Dashboard.

⑥ Use the mouse (🐦) to click and drag the widget to the position you prefer.

Ⓑ If the widget is configurable, it displays an *i* when you position the mouse (🐦) over it.

⑦ Click the *i*.

⑧ Configure the widget as needed.

⑨ Click **Done**.

⑩ Click **Exit** (◉).

Your Mac closes the Dashboard.

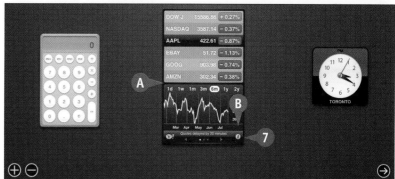

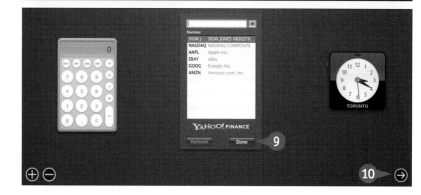

TIPS

Are there other methods I can use to open the Dashboard?

Yes. You can open and close the Dashboard quickly on most Macs by pressing F12 (or Fn+F12). On most Apple keyboards, you can also press F4 to open and close the Dashboard.

How do I remove a widget from the Dashboard?

To remove a single widget, press and hold Option, position the mouse (🐦) over the widget, and then click the **Close** button (◉) that the Dashboard displays in the upper-left corner of the widget. To remove more than one widget, click ◉ and then click ◉ in each widget that you want to remove.

Extend the Desktop Across Multiple Displays

You can improve your productivity and efficiency by connecting a second monitor to your Mac. To work with an extra display, your Mac must have a video output port — such as a Thunderbolt port, Mini DisplayPort, or DVI port — that matches a corresponding port on the second display. If you do not have such a port, check with Apple or the display manufacturer to see if an adapter is available that enables your Mac to connect with the second display. After you connect your Mac to the display, you can extend the OS X desktop across both monitors.

Extend the Desktop Across Multiple Displays

1 Connect the second monitor to your Mac.

2 In the Dock, click **System Preferences** (⚙).

The System Preferences window appears.

3 Click **Displays**.

The Displays preferences appear.

4 Click **Arrangement**.

Ⓐ This window represents your Mac's main display.

Ⓑ This window represents the second display.

Ⓒ This white strip represents the OS X menu bar.

5 Click and drag the windows to set the relative arrangement of the two displays.

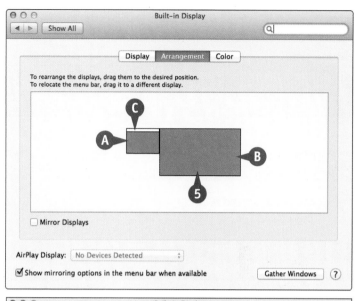

6 To move the menu bar and Dock to the second display, click and drag the menu bar and drop it on the second display.

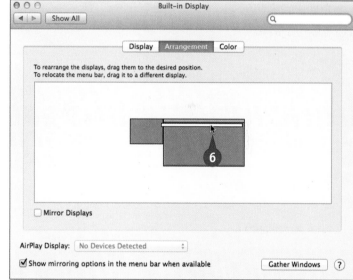

Can I use a different desktop background in each display?

Yes. To set the desktop background on the second display, open System Preferences and click **Desktop & Screen Saver**. On the second display, you see the Secondary Desktop dialog. Use that dialog to set the desktop picture or color, as described in the section "Change the Desktop Background."

Can I just use the second display to show my main OS X desktop?

Yes. This is called *mirroring* the main display because the second display shows exactly what appears on your Mac's main monitor, including the mouse pointer. Follow steps **1** to **4** to display the Arrangement tab, then click **Mirror Displays** (☐ changes to ☑).

CHAPTER 13

Maintaining OS X

To keep OS X running smoothly, maintain top performance, and reduce the risk of computer problems, you need to perform some routine maintenance chores. This chapter shows you how to empty the Trash, delete unnecessary files, uninstall applications, back up and restore your files, recondition your notebook battery, and more.

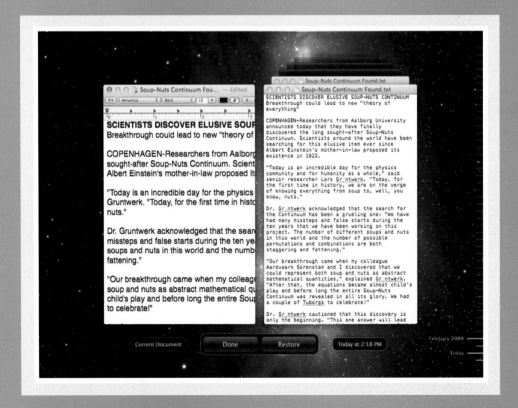

Empty the Trash

You can free up disk space on your Mac by periodically emptying the Trash. When you delete a file or folder, OS X does not immediately remove the file from your Mac's hard drive. Instead, OS X moves the file or folder to the Trash. This is useful if you accidentally delete an item, because it means you can open the Trash and restore the item. However, all those deleted files and folders take up disk space, so you need to empty the Trash periodically to regain that space. You should empty the Trash at least once a week.

Empty the Trash

1 Click the desktop.

2 Click **Finder** from the menu.

3 Click **Empty Trash**.

A You can also right-click the **Trash** icon (🗑) and then click **Empty Trash**.

Note: Another way to select the Empty Trash command is to press **Shift** + **⌘** + **Delete**.

OS X asks you to confirm the deletion.

4 Click **Empty Trash**.

OS X empties the Trash (🗑 changes to 🗑).

262

Organize Your Desktop

You can make your OS X desktop easier to scan and navigate by organizing the icons. The OS X desktop automatically displays icons for objects such as your external hard drives, inserted CDs and DVDs, disk images, and attached iPods. The desktop is also a handy place to store files, file aliases, copies of documents, and more. However, the more you use your desktop as a storage area, the more the desktop can become disarrayed, making it hard to find the icon you want. You can fix this by organizing the icons.

Organize Your Desktop

1 Click the desktop.

2 Click **View**.

3 Click **Clean Up By**.

4 Click **Name**.

You can also right-click the desktop, click **Clean Up By**, and then click **Name**, or press `Option`+`⌘`+`1`.

A Your Mac organizes the icons alphabetically and arranges them in columns from right to left.

Check Hard Drive Free Space

To ensure that your Mac's hard drive does not become full, you should periodically check how much free space it has left. If you run out of room on your Mac's hard drive, you will not be able to install more applications or create more documents, and your Mac's performance will suffer. To ensure your free space does not become too low — say, less than about 20 or 25GB — you can check how much free space your hard drive has left.

You should check your Mac's hard drive free space about once a month.

Check Hard Drive Free Space

Check Free Space Using Finder

1 Click **Finder** (🏃).

2 Click **Desktop**.

Note: You can also click any folder on your Mac's hard drive.

3 In the status bar, read the available value, which tells you the amount of free space left on the hard drive.

If you do not see the status bar, press ⌘+/.

Display Free Space on the Desktop

1 Display your Mac's HD (hard drive) icon on the desktop, as described in the first Tip.

2 Click the desktop.

3 Click **View**.

4 Click **Show View Options**.

Note: You can also run the Show View Options command by pressing ⌘+J.

The Desktop dialog appears.

5 Click **Show item info**
(☐ changes to ☑).

A Your Mac displays the amount
of free hard drive space under
the Macintosh HD icon.

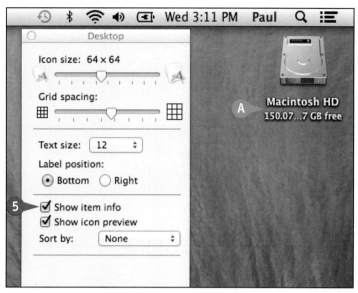

6 Drag the Icon size ♡ until
you can read all the icon text.

7 If you still cannot read all
the text, click the **Text size** ⧨
and then click a larger size.

8 Click **Close** (◯).

TIPS

My Mac's hard drive icon does not appear on the desktop. How do I display it?

If you do not see the Macintosh HD icon on your desktop, click the desktop, click **Finder** in the menu bar, and then click **Preferences**. Click the **General** tab, click **Hard disks** (☐ changes to ☑), and then click **Close** (◯).

What should I do if my Mac's hard drive space is getting low?

First, empty the Trash, as described earlier in this chapter. Next, uninstall applications you no longer use, as described in the next section. If you have large documents you no longer need, either move them to an external hard drive or flash drive, or delete them and then empty the Trash.

Uninstall Unused Applications

If you have an application that you no longer use, you can free up some disk space and reduce clutter in the Applications folder by uninstalling that application. When you install an application, the program stores its files on your Mac's hard drive, and although most programs are quite small, many require hundreds of megabytes of space. Uninstalling applications you do not need frees up the disk space they use and removes their icons or folders from the Applications folder. In most cases, you must be logged on to OS X with an administrator account to uninstall applications.

Uninstall Unused Applications

1 Click **Finder** ( ).

2 Click **Applications**.

3 Click and drag the application or its folder and drop it on the **Trash** icon (🗑).

If your Mac prompts you for an administrator password, type the password, and then click **OK**.

A Your Mac uninstalls the application.

TIP

Is there another way to uninstall an application?

Yes, in some cases. A few Mac applications come with a separate program for uninstalling the application:

1 Follow steps **1** and **2**.

2 Open the application's folder, if it has one.

3 Double-click the Uninstaller icon and then follow the instructions on-screen.

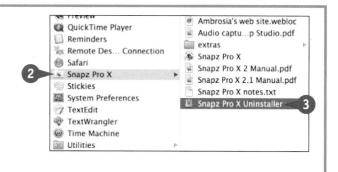

Force a Stuck Application to Close

When you are working with an application, you may find that it becomes unresponsive and you cannot interact with the application or even quit the application normally. In that case, you can use an OS X feature called Force Quit to force a stuck or unresponsive application to close, which enables you to restart the application or restart your Mac.

Unfortunately, when you force an application to quit, you lose any unsaved changes in your open documents. Therefore, you should make sure the application really is stuck before forcing it to quit. See the second Tip for more information.

Force a Stuck Application to Close

1 Click .

2 Click **Force Quit**.

The Force Quit Applications
window appears.

3 Click the application you
want to shut down.

4 Click **Force Quit**.

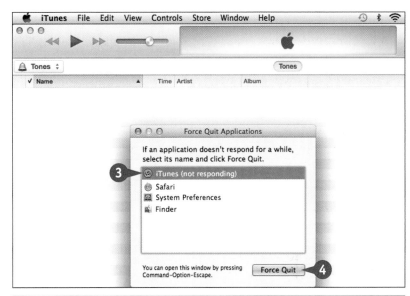

Your Mac asks you to confirm
that you want to force the
application to quit.

5 Click **Force Quit**.

Your Mac shuts down the
application.

6 Click **Close** (⬤) to close
the Force Quit Applications
window.

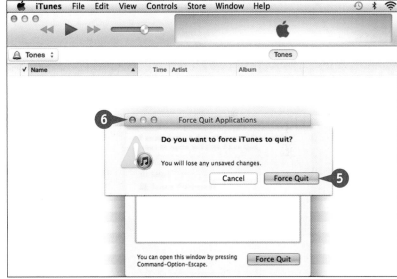

TIPS

**Are there easier ways to run the Force
Quit command?**

Yes. From the keyboard, run the Force Quit
command by pressing `Option`+`⌘`+`Esc`. If
the application has a Dock icon, press and
hold `Control`+`Option` and then click the
application's Dock icon. In the menu that
appears, click **Force Quit**.

**If an application is not responding, does that always
mean the application is stuck?**

Not necessarily. Some operations — such as recalculating a
large spreadsheet or rendering a 3-D image — can take a few
minutes, and during that time the application can appear
stuck. If your Mac is low on memory, it can also cause an
application to seem stuck. In this case, try shutting down
some of other applications to free up some memory.

Configure Time Machine Backups

One of the most crucial OS X maintenance chores is to configure your system to make regular backups of your files. Macs are reliable machines, but they can crash and all hard drives eventually die, so at some point your data will be at risk. To avoid losing that data forever, you need to configure Time Machine to perform regular backups.

To use Time Machine, your Mac requires a second hard drive. This can be a second internal drive on a Mac Pro or Mac mini, but on most Macs the easiest course is to connect an external hard drive.

Configure Time Machine Backups

Configure Backups Automatically

1 Connect an external USB, Thunderbolt, or FireWire hard drive to your Mac.

OS X asks if you want to use the hard drive as your backup disk.

2 Click **Use as Backup Disk**.

Note: If OS X does not ask to use the hard drive, continue with the following steps.

Configure Backups Manually

1 Click **System Preferences** (⬚).

2 Click **Time Machine**.

The Time Machine preferences appear.

3 Click **Select Backup Disk**.

Time Machine displays a list of available backup devices.

4 Click the external hard drive.

5 Click **Use Disk**.

Time Machine enables backups and prepares to run the first backup automatically in 2 minutes.

6 Click **Close** (⬤).

TIP

How do Time Machine backups work?

Time Machine backups are handled automatically as follows:

- The initial backup occurs 2 minutes after you configure Time Machine for the first time. This backup includes your entire Mac.

- Another backup runs every hour. These hourly backups include files and folders you have changed or created since the most recent hourly backup.

- Time Machine runs a daily backup that includes only those files and folders that you have changed or created since the most recent daily backup.

- Time Machine runs a weekly backup that includes only those files and folders that you have changed or created since the most recent weekly backup.

Restore an Earlier Version of a File

If you improperly edit or accidentally overwrite a file, some apps enable you to revert to an earlier version of the file. Why would you want to revert to an earlier version of a file? One reason is that you might improperly edit the file by deleting or changing important data. In some cases you may be able to restore that data by going back to a previous version of the file. Similarly, if you overwrite the file with a different file, you can fix the problem by restoring an earlier version of the file.

Restore an Earlier Version of a File

1 Open the file you want to restore.

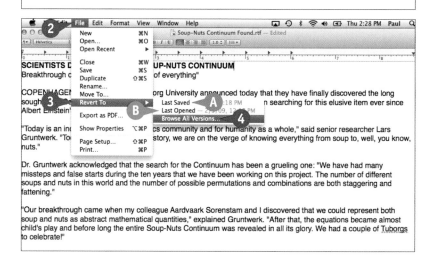

2 Click **File**.

3 Click **Revert To**.

Note: If you do not see the Revert To command, it means the application does not support this feature.

Ⓐ To restore the most recently saved version, click **Last Saved**.

Ⓑ To restore the most recently opened version, click **Last Opened**.

4 Click **Browse All Versions**.

The restore interface appears.

C This window represents the current version of the file.

D Each of these windows represents an earlier version of the file.

E This area tells you when the displayed version of the file was saved.

F You can use this timeline to navigate the earlier versions.

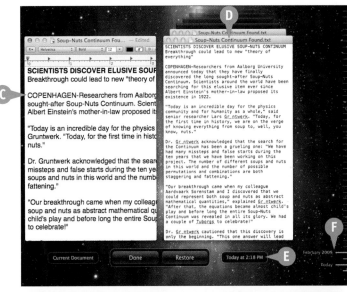

5 Navigate to the date that contains the version of the file you want to restore.

Note: See the Tip to learn how to navigate the Time Machine backups.

6 Click **Restore**.

OS X reverts the file to the earlier version.

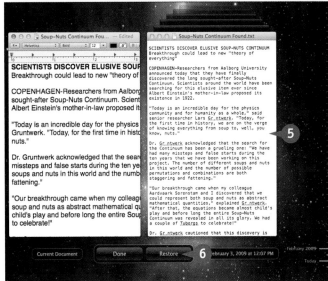

How do I navigate the previous versions?

There are two methods you can use:

- Use the timeline on the right side of the window to click a specific version.
- Click the title bars of the version windows.

Can I restore a previous version without overwriting the current version of the file?

Yes, you can restore a copy of the file. This is useful if the current version has data you want to preserve, or if you want to compare the current version with the earlier version. Follow steps **1** to **5** to navigate to the version of the file that you want to restore. Press and hold the Option key, then click **Restore a Copy**.

Restore Files Using Time Machine

I f you have configured OS X to make regular Time Machine backups, you can use those backups to restore a lost file. If you accidentally delete a file, you can quickly restore it by opening the Trash folder. However, that does not help you if you have emptied the Trash folder. Similarly, if the program or OS X crashes, a file may become corrupted.

Because Time Machine makes hourly, daily, and weekly backups, it stores older copies of your data. You can use these backups to restore any file that you accidentally delete or that has become corrupted.

Restore Files Using Time Machine

1 Click **Finder** ( ).

2 Open the folder you want to restore, or the folder that contains the file you want to restore.

A To restore your entire hard drive, choose **Macintosh HD** in the sidebar.

Note: Restore your entire hard drive only if your original hard drive crashed and you have had it repaired or replaced.

3 Click **Spotlight** (Q).

4 Type **time machine**.

5 Click **Time Machine**.

The Time Machine interface appears.

B Each window represents a backed-up version of the folder.

C This area tells you when the displayed version of the folder was backed up.

D You can use this timeline to navigate the backed-up versions.

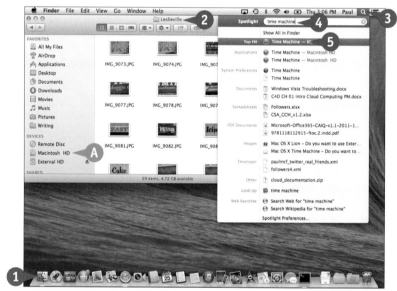

6 Navigate to the date that contains the backed-up version of the folder or file.

Note: See the Tip to learn how to navigate the Time Machine backups.

7 If you are restoring a file, click the file.

8 Click **Restore**.

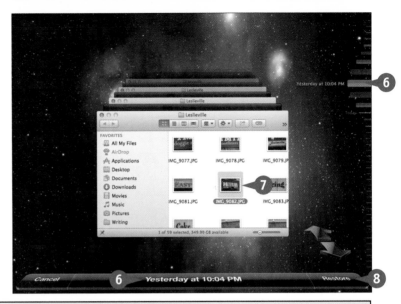

If another version of the folder or file already exists, Time Machine asks if you want to keep it or replace it.

9 Click **Replace**.

Time Machine restores the folder or file.

How do I navigate the backups in the Time Machine interface?

Here are the most useful techniques:

- Click the top arrow to jump to the earliest version; click the bottom arrow to return to the most recent version.
- Press and hold the ⌘ key and click the arrows to navigate through the backups one version at a time.
- Use the timeline to click a specific version.
- Click the version windows.

Recondition Your Mac Notebook Battery

To get the most performance out of your Mac notebook's battery, you need to recondition the battery by cycling it. *Cycling* a battery means letting it completely discharge and then fully recharging it again. Most Mac notebook batteries slowly lose their charging capacity over time. For example, if you can use your Mac notebook on batteries for 4 hours today, you will later be able to run the computer for 3 hours only on a full charge. You cannot stop this process, but you can delay it significantly by cycling the battery once a month or so.

Recondition Your Mac Notebook Battery

Display the Battery Status Percentage

1 Click the **Battery status** icon (⛛).

2 Click **Show Percentage**.

Your Mac shows the percentage of available battery power remaining.

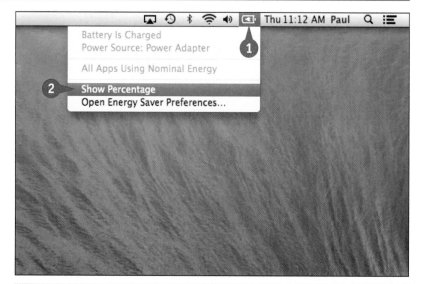

Cycle the Battery

1 Disconnect your Mac notebook's power cord.

A The Battery Status icon changes from ⛛ to ⛛.

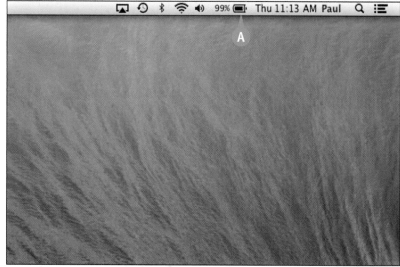

2 Operate your Mac notebook normally by running applications, working with documents, and so on.

3 As you work, keep your eye on the Battery Status percentage.

When the Battery Status reaches 4%, your Mac warns you that it is now running on reserve power.

4 Click **OK**.

5 Reattach the power cord.

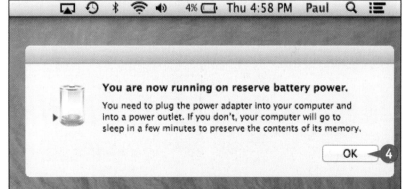

You are now running on reserve battery power.

You need to plug the power adapter into your computer and into a power outlet. If you don't, your computer will go to sleep in a few minutes to preserve the contents of its memory.

OK

Your Mac restarts and the Battery Status icon changes from to .

6 Leave your Mac plugged in at least until the Battery Status shows 100%.

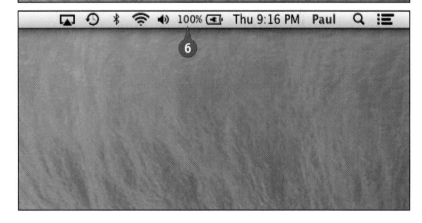

TIP

I do not see the battery status in my menu bar. How do I display it?
Click **System Preferences** (⬜) in the Dock to open System Preferences, and then click the **Energy Saver** icon. In the Energy Saver window, click **Battery** and then click the **Show battery status in the menu bar** check box (☐ changes to ☑).

Restart Your Mac

If a hardware device is having a problem with some system files, it often helps to restart your Mac. By rebooting the computer, you reload the entire system, which is often enough to solve many computer problems.

For a problem device that does not have its own power switch, restarting your Mac might not resolve the problem because the device remains powered up the whole time. You can *power cycle* — shut down and then restart — such devices as a group by power cycling your Mac.

Restart Your Mac

Restart Your Mac

1 Click the **Apple** icon (🍎).

2 Click **Restart**.

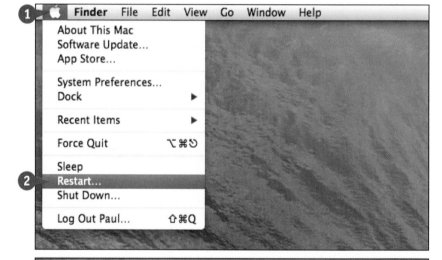

Your Mac asks you to confirm.

3 Click **Restart**.

Note: To bypass the confirmation dialog, press and hold Option when you click the **Restart** command.

Power Cycle Your Mac

1. Click .

2. Click **Shut Down**.

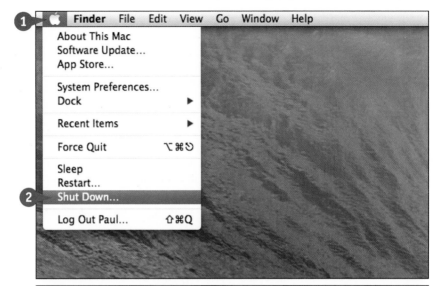

Your Mac asks you to confirm.

Note: To bypass the confirmation dialog, hold down `Option` when you click **Shut Down**.

3. Click **Shut Down**.

4. Wait for 30 seconds to give all devices time to spin down.

5. Turn your Mac back on.

TIP

What other basic troubleshooting techniques can I use?

- Make sure that each device is turned on, that cable connections are secure, and that insertable devices (such as USB devices) are properly inserted.

- If a device is battery powered, replace the batteries.

- If a device has an on/off switch, power cycle the device by turning it off, waiting a few seconds for it to stop spinning, and then turning it back on again.

- Close all running programs.

- Log out of your Mac — click ; click **Log Out *User***, where *User* is your Mac username; and then click **Log Out** — and then log back in again.

CHAPTER 14

Working with Your iCloud Account

You can get a free iCloud account, which is a web-based service that gives you e-mail, an address book, and a calendar. You can also use iCloud to automatically synchronize data between iCloud and your Mac (as well as your iPhone, iPad, or iPod touch).

Create an Apple ID

To use iCloud, you need to create a free Apple ID, which you use to sign in to iCloud on the web and to synchronize your Mac and other devices. An Apple ID is an e-mail address. You can use an existing e-mail address for your Apple ID, or you can sign up for a new iCloud e-mail address, which uses the icloud.com domain name. If you use an existing e-mail address, you are required to verify via e-mail that the address is legitimate.

Create an Apple ID

1 Click **System Preferences** (⚙).

The System Preferences window appears.

2 Click **iCloud**.

The iCloud preferences appear.

3 Click **Create an Apple ID**.

The Create an Apple ID dialog appears.

④ Click the **Location** pop-up menu and choose your country.

⑤ Click the three **Birthday** pop-up menus and choose your month, day, and year of birth.

⑥ Click **Next**.

⑦ Select **Get a free iCloud email address** (○ changes to ⊙).

Ⓐ If you prefer to use an existing address, select **Use an existing email address** (○ changes to ⊙) instead.

⑧ Type the address.

⑨ Type your name.

⑩ Type the password.

⑪ Click **Next**.

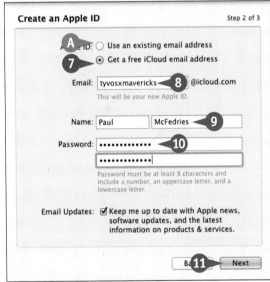

TIP

If I do not want to create a new iCloud address, can I use any e-mail address?
Yes, as long as the address belongs to you. Also, you need to be able to retrieve and read messages that are sent to that address, as this is part of the verification process. To learn how to verify an existing address that you entered in step **8**, see the tip at the end of the section "Create an Apple ID."

continued ▶

Create an Apple ID (continued)

As part of the sign-up process, you specify which iCloud services to use. First, you decide whether you want to synchronize data such as contacts, calendars, and bookmarks with iCloud. If you are not sure, you can turn this feature off for now, and decide later (see the section "Set Up iCloud Synchronization"). Second, you decide whether you want to use Find My Mac, which enables you to use iCloud to locate your lost or stolen Mac. Again, if you are not sure what to do, you can decide later (see the section "Locate a Lost Mac, iPod, iPhone, or iPad").

Create an Apple ID (continued)

12 For each security question, click ‡ to select a question and then type an answer.

13 If you want to supply Apple with an emergency e-mail address, type it in the Rescue Email box.

14 Click **Next**.

15 Select the **I have read and agree to the iCloud Terms of Service** check box (☐ changes to ☑).

16 Click **Continue**.

OS X prompts you to choose which iCloud services you want to use.

17 If you do not want to sync your data to iCloud, click **Use iCloud for contacts, calendars, and bookmarks** (☑ changes to ☐).

18 If you do not want to use iCloud to locate your Mac, click **Use Find My Mac** (☑ changes to ☐).

19 Click **Next**.

If you elected to use Find My Mac, OS X asks you to confirm.

20 Click **Allow**.

OS X sets up your iCloud account on your Mac.

Note: If you have trouble enabling Find My Mac, see the Tip in the section "Locate a Lost Mac, iPod, iPhone, or iPad."

TIP

What happens after I create my Apple ID from an existing address?

After you agree to the terms of service, Apple sends an e-mail message to the address you typed in step **8**. When that message arrives, open it and click the verification link. In the web page that appears, type your Apple ID (that is, the e-mail address from step **8**), type your password, and then click **Verify Address**. Return to the iCloud preferences, click **Next**, and then follow steps **15** to **20**.

Sign In to iCloud

Before you can use the features associated with your iCloud account, you must sign in to the service. iCloud is a web-based service, so you access it using a web browser. Most modern browsers should work fine with iCloud, but Apple recommends that you use at least Safari 6, Firefox 16, Internet Explorer 9, or Chrome 23.

You can also sign in to iCloud using a Mac, and for that you must be using OS X Lion 10.7.5 or later. You can also access iCloud using a Windows PC, and in this case the PC must be running Windows 8, Windows 7, or Windows Vista with Service Pack 2 or later.

Sign In to iCloud

1 In your web browser, type **www.icloud.com**.

2 Press **Return**.

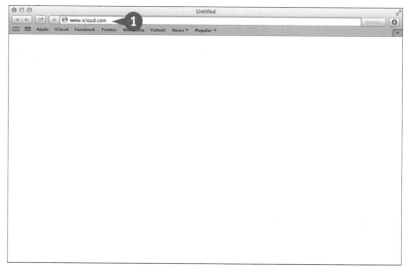

The iCloud Login page appears.

3 Use the Apple ID text box to type your Apple ID.

4 Use the Password text box to type the password for your Apple ID.

Ⓐ If you want iCloud to sign you in automatically in the future, click **Remember me in** (☐ changes to ☑).

⑤ Click **Sign In** (→).

The first time you sign in, iCloud prompts you to configure some settings.

⑥ Click **Add Photo**, drop a photo on the dialog that appears, and then click **Done**.

⑦ Click **Done.**

TIPS

Can I sign in from my Mac?
Yes. Click **System Preferences** (⚙) in the Dock (or click and then click **System Preferences**) and then click **iCloud**. Type your Apple ID and password and then click **Sign In**.

How do I sign out from iCloud?
When you are done working with your iCloud account, if you prefer not to remain signed in to your account, click the **Sign Out** link beside your account name in the upper-right corner of the iCloud page.

Set Up iCloud Synchronization

You can ensure that your Mac and your iCloud account have the same data by synchronizing the two. The main items you will want to synchronize are Mail e-mail accounts, contacts, calendars, reminders, and notes. However, there are many other types of data you may want to synchronize to iCloud, including Safari bookmarks, photos, and documents. If you have a second Mac, a Windows PC, or an iPhone, iPad, or iPod touch, you can also synchronize it with the same iCloud account, which ensures that your Mac and the device use the same data.

Set Up iCloud Synchronization

1 Click the **Apple** icon (🍎).

2 Click **System Preferences**.

Note: You can also open System Preferences by clicking its icon (📷) on the Dock.

The System Preferences window appears.

3 Click **iCloud**.

The iCloud preferences appear.

④ Select the check box beside a type of data you want to sync (☐ changes to ☑).

Ⓐ OS X sets up the sync.

⑤ Repeat step 4 for each type of data you want to sync.

⑥ If you do not want to sync a type of data, click its check box (☑ changes to ☐).

OS X asks if you want to keep or delete the iCloud data that you are no longer syncing.

⑦ Click here to keep the data on your Mac.

Ⓑ If you do not want to keep the data, click **Delete from Mac**.

Your Mac synchronizes the data with your iCloud account.

TIP

What happens if I modify an appointment, contact, bookmark, or other data in iCloud?
The synchronization process works both ways. That is, all the Mac data you selected to synchronize is sent to your iCloud account. However, the data on your iCloud account is also sent to your Mac. This means that if you modify, add, or delete data on your iCloud account, those changes are also reflected in your Mac data.

Generate a Website Password

You can make it easier and faster to navigate many websites by using Safari to generate, and iCloud to store, passwords for those sites that require you to log in. Many websites require you to set up an account, which means you must log in with a username and password. Good security practices dictate using a unique and hard-to-guess password for each site, but this requires memorizing a large number of passwords. To enhance security and ease Web navigation, you can use Safari to automatically generate for each site a unique and secure password that is stored safely with your iCloud account.

Generate a Website Password

Turn on iCloud Keychain

1. Click **System Preferences** (🖥).

   The System Preferences window appears.

2. Click **iCloud**.

   The iCloud preferences appear.

3. Select the **Keychain** check box (☐ changes to ☑).

   OS X prompts you for your Apple ID password.

4. Type your password.

5. Click **OK**.

   OS X activates iCloud Keychain.

Generate a Website Password

1 In Safari, navigate to a web page that requires a new password.

2 Click inside the password field.

A Safari displays its suggested password.

3 Click the password.

OS X asks if you want to keep or delete the iCloud data that you are no longer syncing.

Use a Generated Website Password

1 In Safari, navigate to a web page that requires you to log in using a previously generated password.

2 Begin typing the username.

B Safari displays the full username.

3 Click **Use password from "website"**, where *website* is the name of the site.

Safari fills in the website password.

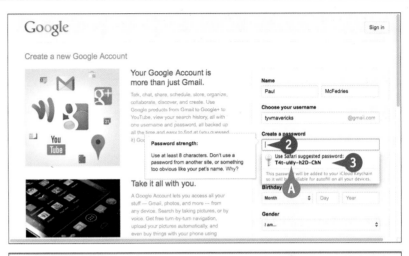

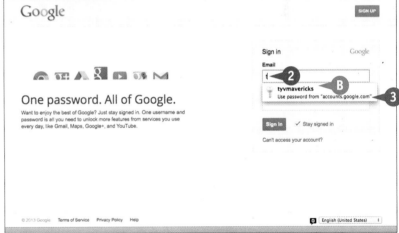

What is iCloud Keychain?

A *keychain* is a master list of usernames and passwords that a system stores for easy access by an authorized user. iCloud Keychain is a special type of keychain that stores website passwords auto-generated by Safari. This means that you do not have to remember these passwords because Safari can automatically retrieve them from your iCloud account. Even better, any Mac or iOS device such as an iPhone or iPad that uses the same iCloud account has access to the same keychain, so your website passwords also work on those devices. On the downside, this sets up a possible security problem should you lose your iPhone or iPad. Therefore, be sure to configure your device with a passcode lock to prevent unauthorized access to your iCloud Keychain.

Send and Receive iCloud Mail

You can use the iCloud Mail feature to work with your iCloud e-mail account online. Using either your Mac or any computer or device with web access, you can access iCloud using a web browser and then perform your e-mail tasks. These include checking for incoming messages, replying to messages you receive, forwarding a received message, and composing and sending a new message. You can also configure iCloud Mail to send blind courtesy copies and to automatically send vacation messages.

Send and Receive iCloud Mail

Display iCloud Mail

1 Sign in to your iCloud account.

Note: See the section "Sign In to iCloud" earlier in this chapter.

2 If you are using another section of iCloud, click **iCloud** (not shown).

3 Click **Mail** (▢).

Get Incoming Messages

1 Click **Get Mail** (↻).

Ⓐ iCloud Mail checks for incoming messages and, if there are any, displays them in the Inbox folder.

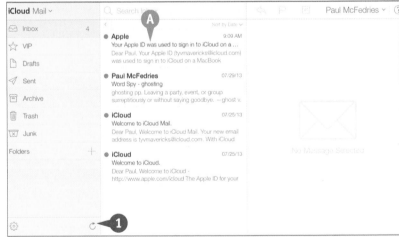

Reply to a Message

1. Click the message.

2. Click **Reply, Reply All, Forward** (↩).

3. Click **Reply**.

4. In the message window that appears (not shown), type your message and then click **Send**.

Send a New Message

1. Click **Compose new message** (✐).

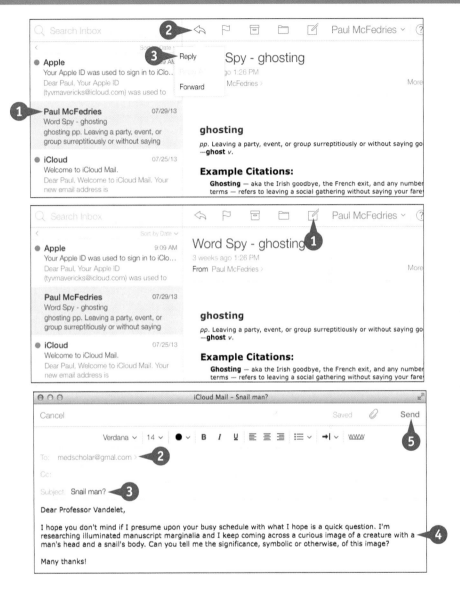

The New Message window appears.

2. Click the **To** text box and type the recipient's e-mail address.

3. Click the **Subject** text box and type the subject of the message.

4. Type your message.

5. Click **Send**.

Can I use iCloud to send a message to a person without other recipients knowing?

Yes, you can send that person a blind courtesy copy (Bcc), which means that he or she receives a copy of the message, but the other message recipients do not see that person's name or address in the recipient fields. To activate this feature, open iCloud Mail, click **Actions** (⚙), click **Preferences**, and then click the **Composing** tab. Click **Show Bcc field** (☐ changes to ☑) and then click **Done**.

Work with iCloud Contacts

You can use iCloud to store information about your friends, family, colleagues, and clients. Using the Contacts app, you can store data such as the person's name, company name, phone numbers, e-mail address, and street address.

The Contacts app also enables you to write notes about a contact, store extra data such as the person's job title and birthday, and assign a picture to a contact. If you already have contacts in your Mac's Contacts app, you can synchronize them with iCloud. See the section "Set Up iCloud Synchronization" earlier in this chapter.

Work with iCloud Contacts

Display iCloud Contacts

① Click **iCloud**.

② Click **Contacts** (👤).

Create a Contact

① Click **Create a new contact** (+).

② Click **New Contact**

③ Type the person's first name and last name.

④ Type the person's company's name.

⑤ Click here and then click a phone number category.

⑥ Type the phone number.

⑦ Click an e-mail category.

⑧ Type the person's e-mail address.

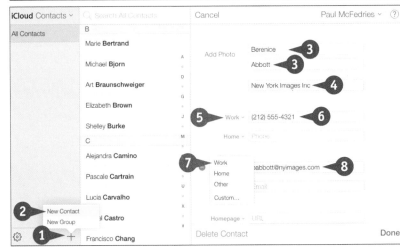

294

9 Click **Add new address** (not shown).

10 Click a street address category.

11 Use the text boxes in this section to type the person's street address.

12 Click **Done**.

iCloud saves the contact.

Display a Contact

1 Use the scroll bar to locate the contact.

2 Click the contact.

A iCloud displays the contact's details.

B You can also type part of the contact's name in the Search box.

C To e-mail the contact, click the address.

D To make changes to the contact, click **Edit**.

To remove the contact, click **Edit** and then click **Delete Contact**.

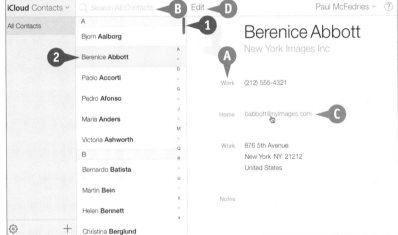

How do I add a photo for a contact?
Click the contact, click **Edit**, click **Add Photo** and then drag a photo to the dialog that appears. Alternatively, click **Choose Photo**, click the photo you want to use, and then click **Choose**. Click **Done**. Note that you can use only GIF, JPEG, or PNG files that are no larger than 1MB.

Is there any way to store data such as the person's birthday or job title?
Yes. To add a field to an existing contact, click the contact and then click **Edit**. Click **Add Field**, click the field you want, and then enter the field data.

Manage Your Schedule with iCloud

You can use iCloud to manage your schedule. Using the Calendar application, you can add events (appointments and all-day activities) and reminders. For events, you can specify the date and time they occur, the event name and location, and notes related to the event.

You can also use the Calendar application to display your schedule by day, by week, or by month. If you already have events in your OS X Calendar application, you can synchronize them with iCloud. See the section "Set Up iCloud Synchronization" earlier in this chapter.

Manage Your Schedule with iCloud

Display iCloud Calendar

1 Click **iCloud**.

2 Click **Calendar** ( ).

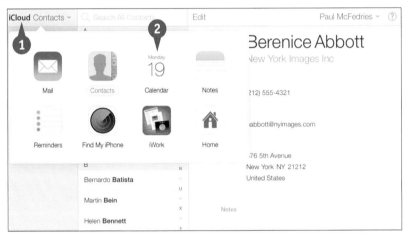

Navigate Calendar

1 Click **Month**.

2 Click **Next Month** (>) and **Previous Month** (<) to select the month you want.

3 Click the date.

Ⓐ To see just that date, click **Day**.

Ⓑ To see the date in the context of its week, click **Week**.

Ⓒ To return to today's date, click **Go to today**.

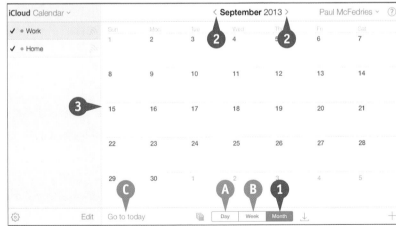

Create an Event

1 Navigate to the date when the event occurs.

2 Click the calendar you want to use.

3 Click **Week**.

4 Position the ▲ at the time when the event starts.

5 Click and drag the ▲ down to the time when the event ends.

Ⓓ Calendar adds the event.

6 Type the event name.

7 Type the event location.

Ⓔ If the event lasts all day, click **all-day** (☐ changes to ☑).

8 Adjust the start time, if necessary.

9 Adjust the end time, if necessary.

10 Fill in the other event details as needed.

11 Click **OK**.

Note: To edit the event, double-click it.

TIP

How do I create a reminder?

1 Click **iCloud**.

2 Click **Reminders** ( ).

3 Click **New Item**.

4 Type the reminder name.

5 Click **Details**.

6 Fill in the rest of the reminder details as needed.

7 Click **Done**.

Locate and Lock a Lost Mac, iPod, iPhone, or iPad

You can use iCloud to locate a lost or stolen Mac, iPod touch, iPhone, or iPad. Depending on how you use your Mac, iPod touch, iPhone, or iPad, you can end up with many details of your life residing on the device. That is generally a good thing, but if you happen to lose your device, you have also lost those details, plus you have created a large privacy problem because anyone can now see your data. You can locate your device and even remotely lock the device using an iCloud feature called Find My iPhone, which also works for Macs, iPod touches, and iPads.

Locate and Lock a Lost Mac, iPod, iPhone, or iPad

1 Click **iCloud**.

2 Click **Find My iPhone** (⬤).

Note: If iCloud asks you to sign in to your account, type your password and click **Sign In**.

3 Click **All Devices**.

4 Click the device you want to locate.

A iCloud displays the device location on a map.

5 Click **Lost Mode**.

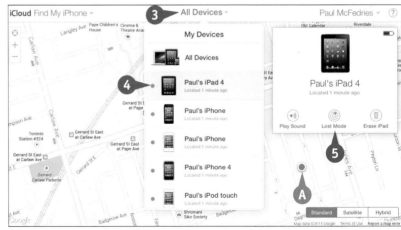

The Lost Mode dialog appears.

⑥ Click a four-digit lock code.

⑦ Enter the lock code again to confirm (not shown).

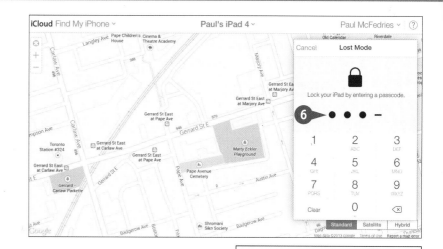

iCloud prompts you to enter a phone number where you can be contacted.

⑧ Type the phone number.

⑨ Click **Next**.

iCloud prompts you to enter a message to display on the device.

⑩ Type your message.

⑪ Click **Done**.

iCloud locks the device and sends the message, which then appears on the device screen.

TIP

I tried to enable Find My Mac, but OS X would not allow it. How can I enable Find My Mac?
You first need to enable location services. To do this, click **System Preferences** (⚙) in the Dock. Click **Security & Privacy**, click the **Lock** icon (🔒), type your OS X administrator password, and then click **OK** (🔒 changes to 🔓). Click **Privacy**, click **Location Services**, and then click **Enable Location Services** (☐ changes to ☑).

CHAPTER 15

Networking with OS X

If you have multiple computers in your home or office, you can set up these computers as a network to share information and equipment. This chapter gives an overview of networking concepts and shows you how to connect to a network, how to work with the other computers on your network, and how to share your Mac's resources with other network users.

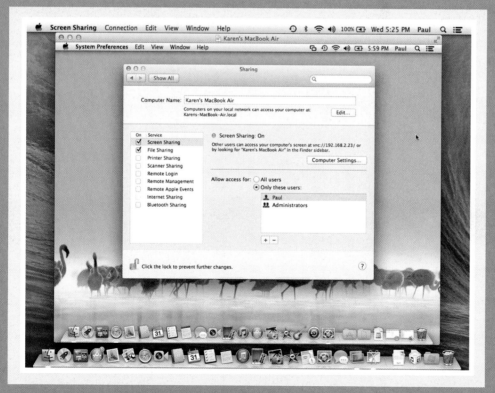

Understanding Networking

A *network* is a collection of computers and other devices that are connected. You can create a network using cable hookups, wireless hookups, or a combination of the two. In both cases, you need special networking equipment to make the connections.

A network gives you a number of advantages. For example, once you have two or more computers connected on a network, those computers can share documents, photos, and other files. You can also use a network to share equipment, such as printers and optical drives.

Share Files

Networked computers are connected to each other, and so they can exchange files with each other along the connection. This enables people to share information and to collaborate on projects. OS X includes built-in security, so that you can control what files you share with other people.

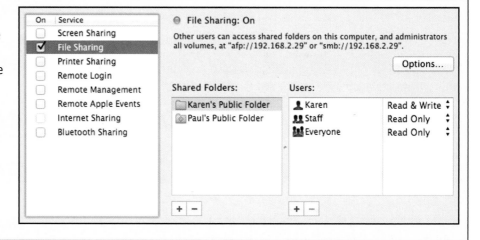

Share Equipment

Computers connected over a network can share some types of equipment. For example, one computer can share its printer, which enables other network users to send their documents to that printer. Networked computers can also share hard drives, optical drives, and document scanners.

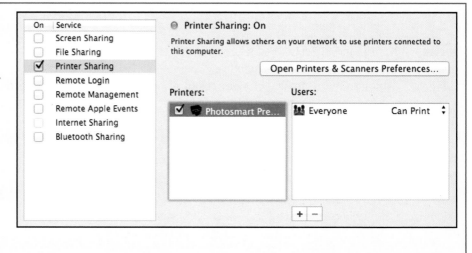

Wired Networking

Network Cable

A *network cable* is a special cable designed for exchanging information. One end of the cable plugs into the Mac's network port, if it has one. The other end plugs into a network connection point, which is usually the network's router (discussed next), but it could also be a switch, hub, or even another Mac. Information, shared files, and other network data travel through the network cables.

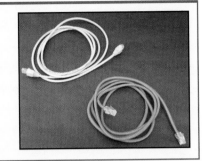

Router

A *router* is a central connection point for all of the computers on the wired portion of the network. For each computer, you run a network cable from the Mac's network port to a port in the router. When network data travels from computer A to computer B, it first goes out through computer A's network port, along its network cable, and into the router. Then the router passes the data along computer B's network cable and into its network port.

Wireless Networking

Wireless Connections

A *wireless network* is a collection of two or more computers that communicate with each other using radio signals instead of cable. The most common wireless technology is Wi-Fi (rhymes with hi-fi) or 802.11. Each of the four main types (802.11ac, 802.11b, 802.11g, and 802.11n) has its own range and speed limits. The other common wireless technology is Bluetooth, which enables devices to communicate directly with each other.

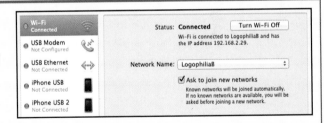

Wireless Access Point

A *wireless access point* (WAP) is a device that receives and transmits signals from wireless computers to form a wireless network. Many WAPs also accept wired connections, which enables both wired and wireless computers to form a network. If your network has a broadband modem, you can connect the modem to a type of WAP called a *wireless gateway,* which includes a built-in router that extends Internet access to all of the computers on the network.

Connect a Bluetooth Device

You can make wireless connections to devices such as mice, keyboards, headsets, and cell phones by using the Bluetooth networking technology. The networking tasks that you learn about in the rest of this chapter require special equipment to connect your computers and devices. However, with Bluetooth devices, the networking is built in, so no extra equipment is needed. For Bluetooth connections to work, your Mac must support Bluetooth (all newer Macs do) and your device must be Bluetooth-enabled. Also, your Mac and the Bluetooth device must remain within about 30 feet of each other.

Connect a Bluetooth Device

Connect a Bluetooth Device without a Passkey

1 Click **System Preferences** ( ) in the Dock.

2 Click **Bluetooth**.

The Bluetooth preferences appear.

3 Click **Turn Bluetooth On**.

OS X activates Bluetooth and makes your Mac discoverable.

④ Perform whatever steps are necessary to make your Bluetooth device discoverable.

For example, if you are connecting a Bluetooth mouse, the device often has a separate switch or button that makes the mouse discoverable, so you need to turn on that switch or press that button.

Ⓐ A list of the available Bluetooth devices appears here.

⑤ Click **Pair** beside the Bluetooth device you want to connect.

⑥ Perform the steps required to pair your Mac and your device.

Ⓑ Your Mac connects with the device.

TIPS

What does it mean to make a device discoverable?

This means that you configure the device to broadcast that it is available for a Bluetooth connection. Controlling the broadcast is important because you usually want to use a Bluetooth device such as a mouse or keyboard with only a single computer.

What does pairing mean?

As a security precaution, many Bluetooth devices do not connect automatically to other devices. This makes sense, because otherwise it means a stranger with a Bluetooth device could connect to your cell phone or even your Mac. To prevent this, most Bluetooth devices require you to type a password before the connection is made. This is known as *pairing* the two devices.

continued ▶ 305

A Bluetooth mouse and a Bluetooth headset do not require any extra pairing steps, although with a headset you must configure OS X to use it for sound output. However, pairing devices such as a Bluetooth keyboard and a Bluetooth cellphone does require an extra step. In most cases, pairing is accomplished by your Mac generating a 6- or 8-digit *passkey* that you must then type into the Bluetooth device (assuming that it has some kind of keypad). In other cases, the device comes with a default passkey that you must type into your Mac to set up the pairing.

Connect a Bluetooth Device (continued)

Connect a Bluetooth Device with a Passkey

1 Turn the device on, if required.

2 Turn on the switch that makes the device discoverable, if required.

3 Follow steps **1** and **2** from earlier in this section to display a list of available Bluetooth devices.

4 Click **Pair** beside your Bluetooth device.

The Bluetooth Setup Assistant displays a passkey.

5 Use the Bluetooth device to type the displayed passkey.

6 Press **Return**.

OS X connects to the device. If you see the Keyboard Setup Assistant, follow the on-screen instructions to set up the keyboard for use with your Mac.

Listen to Audio Through Bluetooth Headphones

1 Click **System Preferences** (■) in the Dock.

2 Click **Sound**.

The Sound preferences appear.

3 Click **Output**.

4 Click the Bluetooth headphones.

TIP

How do I remove a Bluetooth device?

1 Follow steps **1** and **2** under the section "Connect a Bluetooth Device without a Passkey."

2 Position the mouse ▶ over the device you want to disconnect.

3 Click **Disconnect** (⊗).

4 Click **Remove** to remove the device.

Connect to a Wireless Network

All the latest Macs have built-in wireless networking capability that you can use to connect to a wireless network that is within range. This could be a network in your home, your office, or a public location such as a coffee shop. In most cases, this also gives you access to the wireless network's Internet connection.

Most wireless networks have security turned on, which means you must know the correct password to connect to the network. However, after you connect to the network once, your Mac remembers the password and connects automatically the next time the network comes within range.

Connect to a Wireless Network

1 Click the **Wi-Fi status** icon (🛜) in the menu bar.

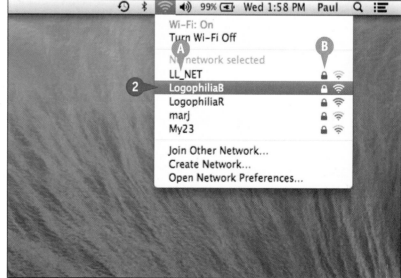

Your Mac locates the wireless networks within range of your Mac.

Ⓐ The available networks appear in the menu.

Ⓑ Networks with a Lock icon (🔒) require a password to join.

2 Click the wireless network you want to join.

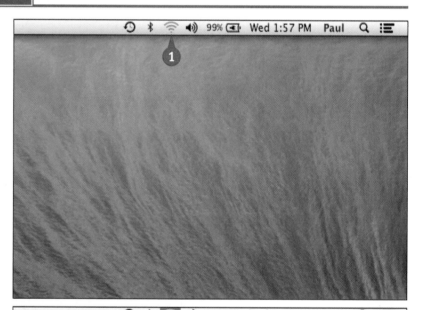

If the wireless network is secure, your Mac prompts you for the password.

③ Use the Password text box to type the network password.

Ⓒ If the password is very long and you are sure no one can see your screen, you can click **Show password** (☐ changes to ☑) to see the actual characters instead of dots. This helps to ensure you type the password correctly.

④ Click **Join**.

Your Mac connects to the wireless network.

Ⓓ The Wi-Fi status icon changes from 📶 to 📶 to indicate the connection.

TIPS

I know a particular network is within range, but I do not see it in the list. Why not?

As a security precaution, some wireless networks do not broadcast their availability. However, you can still connect to such a network, assuming you know its name and the password. Click 📶 and then click **Join Other Network**.

I do not see the Wi-Fi status icon on my menu bar. How do I display the icon?

Click the **System Preferences** icon (🖼) in the Dock (or click 🍎 and then click **System Preferences**) to open the System Preferences window. Click **Network**, click **Wi-Fi**, and then click the **Show Wi-Fi status in menu bar** check box (☐ changes to ☑).

Connect to a Network Resource

To see what other network users have shared on the network, you can use the Network folder to view the other computers and then connect to them to see their shared resources. To get full access to a Mac's shared resources, you must connect with a username and password for an administrator account on that Mac. To get access to the resources that have been shared by a particular user, you must connect with that user's name and password. Note, too, that your Mac can also connect to the resources shared by Windows computers.

Connect to a Network Resource

1 Click the desktop.

2 Click **Go**.

3 Click **Network**.

Note: Another way to run the Network command is to press Shift + ⌘ + K.

The Network folder appears.

A Each icon represents a computer on your local network.

4 Double-click the computer to which you want to connect.

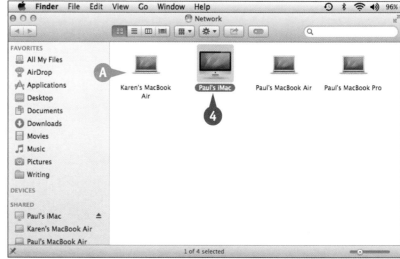

Your Mac connects to the network computer using the Guest account.

Note: The Guest account has only limited access to the network computer.

5 Click **Connect As.**

Your Mac prompts you to connect to the network computer.

6 Click **Registered User** (○ changes to ◉).

7 Type the username of an account on the network computer.

8 Type the password of the account.

9 To store the account data, click **Remember this password in my keychain** (☐ changes to ☑).

10 Click **Connect.**

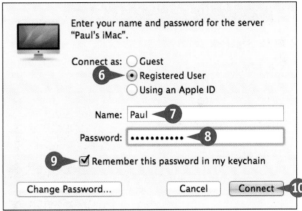

Your Mac connects to the computer and shows the shared resources that you can access.

11 When you are done, click **Disconnect.**

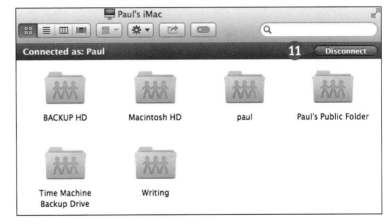

TIP

Is there a faster way to connect to a network computer?
Yes. In the Shared section of Finder's sidebar area, click the computer with which you want to connect (Ⓐ) and then follow steps **5** to **10** to connect as a registered user.

Change Your Password

You can make your Mac more secure by changing your password. For example, if you turn on file sharing, as described in the next section, you can configure each shared folder so that only someone who knows your password can get full access to that folder. Similarly, you should change your password if other network users know your current password and you no longer want them to have access to your shared folders. Finally, you should also change your password if you feel that your current password is not secure enough. See the Tip to learn how to create a secure password.

Change Your Password

1. Click **System Preferences** (🖥️).
2. Click **Users & Groups**.

The Users & Groups preferences appear.

Ⓐ Your user account is selected automatically.

Ⓑ If you want to work with a different user account, you must click the **Lock** icon (🔒) and then type your administrator password (🔒 changes to 🔓).

3. Click **Change Password**.

312

The Change Password dialog appears.

4 Type your current password.

5 Type your new password.

6 Retype the new password.

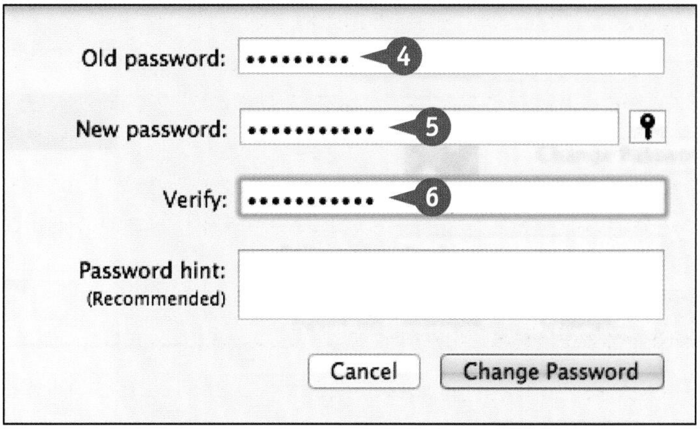

7 Type a hint that OS X will display if you forget the password.

Note: Construct the hint in such a way that it makes it easy for you to recall the password, but hard for a potential snoop to guess the password.

8 Click **Change Password**.

OS X changes your password.

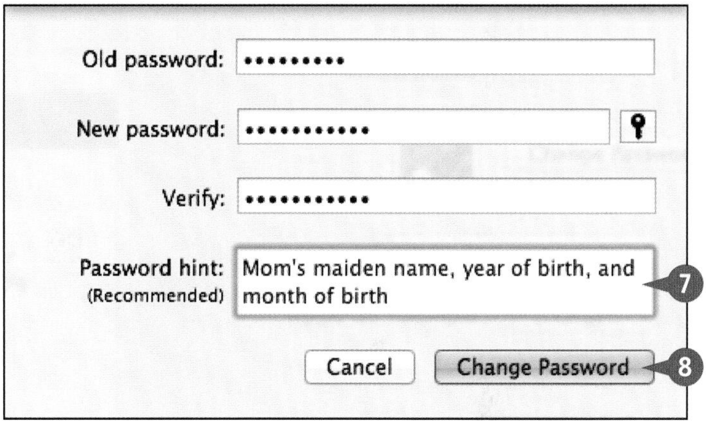

TIP

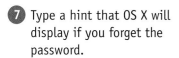

How do I create a secure password?

Follow these steps:

1 Follow steps **1** to **4** in this section.

2 Click the **Password Assistant** icon (🔑).

The Password Assistant dialog appears.

3 Click the **Type** ⬍ and then click a password type.

4 Click and drag the **Length** slider to set the password length you want to use.

5 Click the **Suggestion** down arrow and then click the password you want to use.

6 Click **Close** (●).

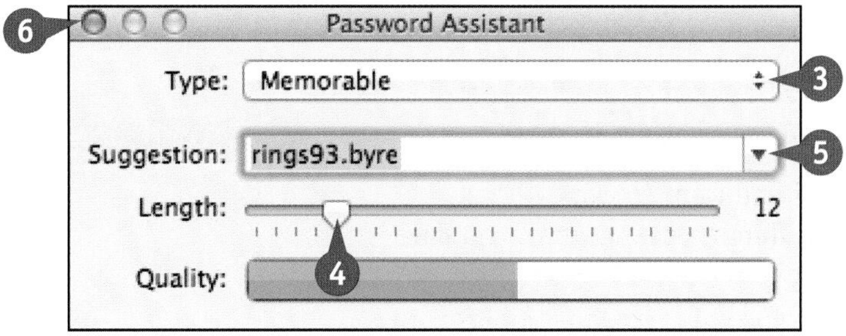

Turn On File and Printer Sharing

You can share your files with other network users. This enables those users to access your files over the network. Before you can share these resources, you must turn on your Mac's file-sharing feature. To learn how to share a particular folder, see the section "Share a Folder" later in this chapter.

You can also share your printer with other network users. This enables those users to send print jobs to your printer over the network. Before this can happen, you must turn on your Mac's printer-sharing feature. To learn how to share a particular printer, see the section "Share a Printer" later in this chapter.

Turn On File and Printer Sharing

1 Click .

2 Click **System Preferences**.

The System Preferences window appears.

3 Click **Sharing**.

The Sharing preferences appear.

④ Click the **File Sharing** check box (☐ changes to ☑).

You can now share your folders, as described in the next section.

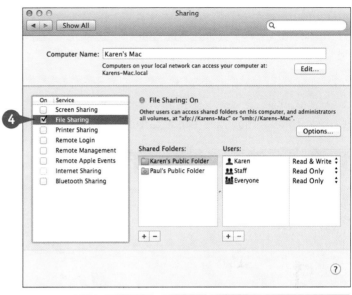

⑤ Click the **Printer Sharing** check box (☐ changes to ☑).

You can now share your printers, as described later in this chapter.

How do I look up my Mac IP address?
In System Preferences, click ◀ to return to the main window, then click **Network**. Click **Wi-Fi** if you have a wireless network connection, or click **Ethernet** if you have a wired connection. In the Status section, read the IP address value.

What is the Public folder and how do I access it?
The Public folder is a special folder for sharing files. Anyone who connects to your Mac using your username and password has full access to the Public folder. To access the folder, click **Finder** (🙂), click **Go**, and then **Home**, and then open the **Public** folder.

Share a Folder

You can share one of your folders on the network, enabling other network users to view and optionally edit the files you place in that folder. OS X automatically shares your user account's Public folder, but you can share other folders. Sharing a folder enables you to work on a file with other people without having to send them a copy of the file. OS X gives you complete control over how people access your shared folder. For example, you can allow users to make changes to the folder, or you can prevent changes.

Share a Folder

1 Open the Sharing preferences.

Note: See the section "Turn On File and Printer Sharing" to learn how to display the Sharing preferences.

2 Click **File Sharing**.

Note: Be sure to click the **File Sharing** text, not the check box. This ensures that you do not accidentally uncheck the check box.

3 Under Shared Folders, click ➕.

An Open dialog appears.

4 Click the folder you want to share.

5 Click **Add**.

Your Mac begins sharing the folder.

Note: You can also click and drag a folder from a Finder window and drop it on the list of shared folders.

A The folder appears in the Shared Folders list.

6 Click the folder.

7 For the Everyone user, click the current permission and then click the permission you want to assign.

B The current permission is indicated with a check mark (✓). OS X assigns the permission to the user.

C You can also click ⊞ under the Users list to add more users.

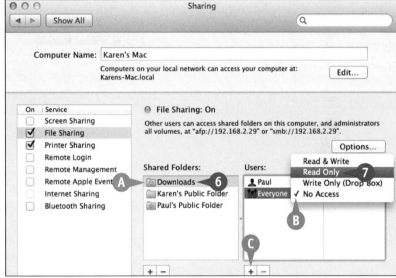

TIPS

What are the differences between the permission types?
Read & Write means users can open files, add new files, rename or delete existing files, and edit file contents. Read Only means users can only open and read files, but cannot add, delete, rename, or edit files. Write Only (Drop Box) means users can add files to the folder as a Drop Box, but cannot open the folder. No Access means users cannot see the folder.

Can I share folders with Windows users?
Yes. In the Sharing window, click **Options** and then click **Share files and folders using SMB (Windows)** (☐ changes to ☑). Click your user account (☐ changes to ☑), type your account password, click **OK**, then click **Done**.

Share a Printer

If you have a printer connected to your Mac, you can share the printer with the network. This enables other network users to send their documents to your printer. Sharing a printer saves you money because you only have to purchase one printer for all the computers on your network. Sharing a printer also saves you time because you only have to install, configure, and maintain a single printer for everyone on your network. See the section "Add a Shared Printer" to learn how to configure OS X to use a shared network printer.

Share a Printer

1 Click .

2 Click **System Preferences**.

Note: You can also click **System Preferences** () in the Dock.

The System Preferences window appears.

3 Click **Sharing**.

④ Click **Printer Sharing**.

Note: Be sure to click the **Printer Sharing** text, not the check box. This ensures that you do not accidentally uncheck the check box.

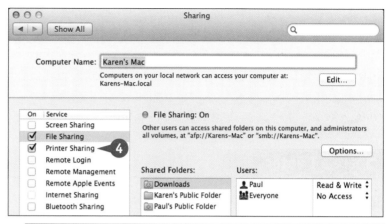

⑤ Click the check box beside the printer you want to share (☐ changes to ☑).

TIP

Is there another method I can use to share a printer?

Yes, you can follow these steps:

① Click .

② Click **System Preferences**.

③ Click **Printers & Scanners**.

④ Click the printer you want to share.

⑤ Click the **Share this printer on the network** check box (☐ changes to ☑).

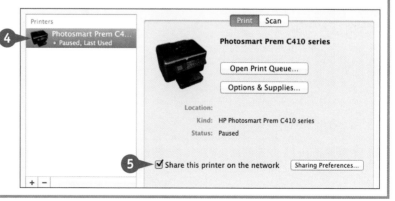

Add a Shared Printer

If another computer on your network has an attached printer that has been shared with the network, you can add that shared printer to your Mac. This enables you to send a document from your Mac to that shared printer, which means you can print your documents without having a printer attached directly to your Mac. Before you can print to a shared network printer, you must add the shared printer to OS X.

Add a Shared Printer

1 Click **System Preferences** ( ) in the Dock.

The System Preferences window appears.

2 Click **Printers & Scanners**.

3 Click .

Note: If OS X displays a list of nearby printers, click the printer you want to add and skip the rest of these steps.

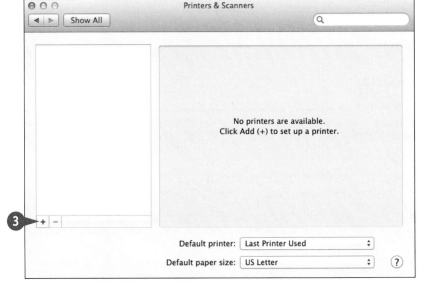

320

④ Click **Default**.

⑤ Click the shared printer.

Ⓐ Look for the word *Shared* in the printer description.

⑥ Click **Add**.

Note: If OS X alerts you that it must install software for the printer, click **Download & Install**.

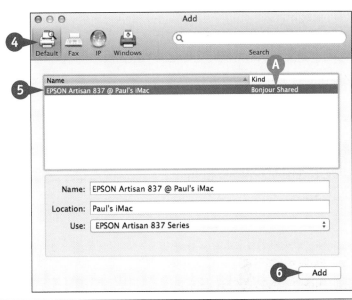

Ⓑ OS X adds the printer.

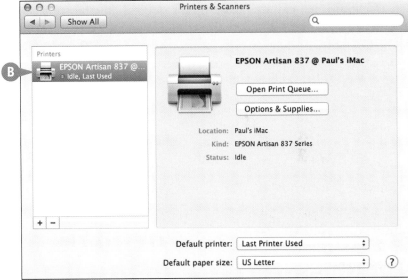

TIPS

TIPS

Can I add a shared Windows printer?
Yes. Follow steps **1** to **3** and then click the **Windows** tab. Click the Windows workgroup, click the computer with the shared printer, log on to the Windows computer, and then click the shared printer you want to use. In the **Print Using** list, click ➕, click **Other**, and then click the printer in the list that appears. Click **Add**.

How do I print to the shared network printer that I added?
In any application that supports printing, click **File** and then click **Print**. In the Print dialog, use the **Printer** pop-up menu to click ➕ and then click the shared printer. Choose any other printing options you require, and then click **Print**.

Share a Screen with Another Mac

You can share your Mac's screen with other computers on your network. Sharing your screen means that everything displayed on your Mac's desktop is also displayed inside a window on the other user's Mac. This is useful for demonstrating something on the screen, because the other user can watch the demonstration without having to be physically present in front of your Mac.

Once you share your screen, the other user can also work with your Mac just as though he or she is sitting in front of it. This is useful if that person needs to troubleshoot a problem.

Share a Screen with Another Mac

Turn On Screen Sharing

1 Open the Sharing preferences.

Note: See the section "Turn On File and Printer Sharing" to learn how to display and unlock the Sharing preferences.

The Sharing preferences appear.

2 Click **Screen Sharing** (☐ changes to ☑).

OS X configures the desktop for sharing.

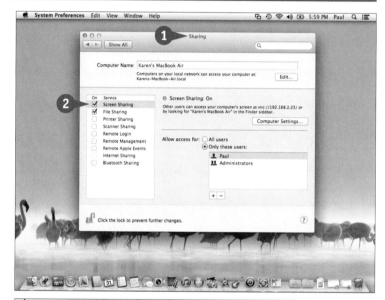

View a Shared Screen

1 On another Mac, click **Finder** (🙂).

2 In the sidebar, click the Mac with the shared screen.

3 Click **Share Screen**.

OS X prompts you to log in to the remote computer.

④ Type the password for an administrative account on the Mac that is sharing the screen.

⑤ Click **Connect**.

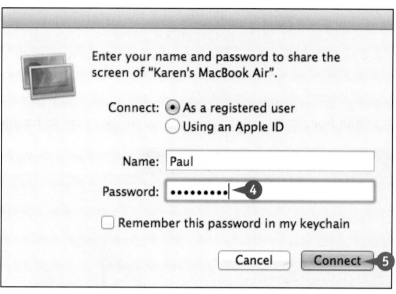

Enter your name and password to share the screen of "Karen's MacBook Air".

Connect: ⦿ As a registered user
◯ Using an Apple ID

Name: Paul

Password: •••••••• ◄ 4

☐ Remember this password in my keychain

Cancel   Connect ◄ 5

Ⓐ OS X displays the shared screen in a window.

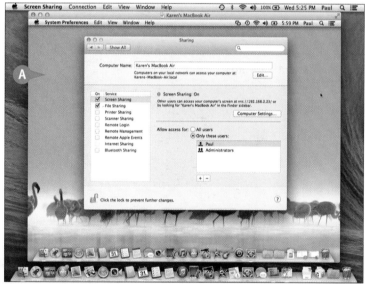

Is it possible to copy data either from or to the Mac with the shared screen?
Yes, you can copy data either way. This is useful if you have text or an image on one Mac and you need to use it on the other. If you want to send data to the Mac with the shared screen, copy the data that you want to send, click **Edit**, and then click **Send Clipboard**. If you want to receive data from the Mac with the shared screen, use that Mac to copy the data that you want to receive. In the Screen Sharing window, click **Edit**, and then click **Get Clipboard**.

View OS X on Your TV

If you have an Apple TV, you can use it to view your OS X screen on your TV. If you want to demonstrate something on your Mac to a group of people, it is difficult because most Mac screens are too small to see from a distance. However, if you have a TV or a projector nearby and you have an Apple TV device connected to that display, you can connect your Mac to the same wireless network and then send the OS X screen to the TV or projector. This is called AirPlay mirroring.

View the OS X Screen on Your TV

Mirror via System Preferences

1 Click **System Preferences** ( ) in the Dock.

The System Preferences window appears.

2 Click **Displays**.

The display preferences appear.

3 Click the **AirPlay Display** and then click your Apple TV.

OS X displays your Mac's screen on your TV.

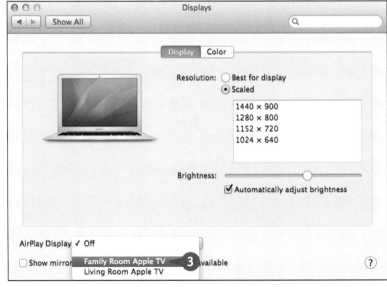

324

Mirror via the Menu Bar

1 Follow steps **1** and **2** to open the display preferences.

2 Click the **Show mirroring options in the menu bar when available** check box (☐ changes to ☑).

Ⓐ OS X adds the AirPlay Mirroring icon (🖵) to the menu bar.

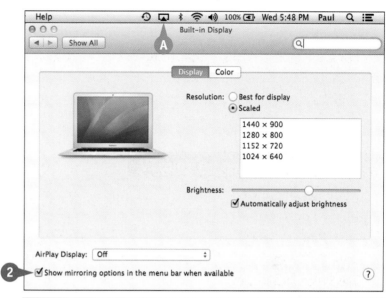

3 Click 🖵.

4 Click your Apple TV.

OS X displays your Mac's screen on your TV (🖵 changes to 🖵).

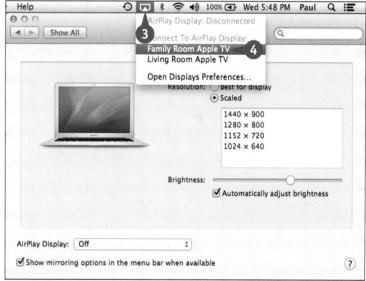

TIPS

Is there an easy way to make my Mac's screen fit my TV screen?
Yes. If you have a high-resolution TV, the OS X screen might look a bit small on the TV. To fix that, click 🖵 and then in the Match Desktop Size To section of the AirPlay Mirroring menu, click your Apple TV.

Can I use my TV as a second monitor for the OS X desktop?
Yes. This is useful if you need extra screen real estate to display the OS X desktop and applications. To configure the TV as a second monitor, click 🖵 and then in the Use AirPlay Display To section of the AirPlay Mirroring menu, click **Extend Desktop**.

Index

329

Read Less-Learn More®

Visual™

There's a Visual book for every learning level...

Simplified®

The place to start if you're new to computers. Full color.

- Computers
- Creating Web Pages
- Digital Photography
- Excel
- Internet
- Laptops
- Mac OS
- Office
- PCs
- Windows
- Word

Teach Yourself VISUALLY™

Get beginning to intermediate-level training in a variety of topics. Full color.

- Access
- Adobe Muse
- Computers
- Digital Photography
- Digital Video
- Dreamweaver
- Excel
- Flash
- HTML5
- iLife
- iPad
- iPhone
- iPod
- Macs
- Mac OS
- Office
- Outlook
- Photoshop
- Photoshop Elements
- Photoshop Lightroom
- PowerPoint
- Salesforce.com
- Search Engine Optimization
- Social Media
- Web Design
- Windows
- Wireless Networking
- Word
- WordPress

Top 100 Simplified® Tips & Tricks

Tips and techniques to take your skills beyond the basics. Full color.

- Digital Photography
- eBay
- Excel
- Google
- Office
- Photoshop
- Photoshop Elements
- PowerPoint
- Windows

...all designed for visual learners—just like you!

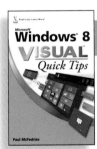

Flexible, fast, and fun, DigitalClassroom.com lets you choose when, where, and how to learn new skills. This subscription-based online learning environment is accessible anytime from your desktop, laptop, tablet, or smartphone. It's easy, efficient learning — on *your* schedule.

- Learn web design and development, Office applications, and new technologies from more than 2,500 video tutorials, e-books, and lesson files
- Master software from Adobe, Apple, and Microsoft
- Interact with other students in forums and groups led by industry pros

Learn more! Sample DigitalClassroom.com for free, now!

We're social. Connect with us!

facebook.com/digitalclassroom
@digitalclassrm